The 33 Principles Every Mason Should Live By:
The True Meaning of Being a Mason

The

33 PRINCIPLES
EVERY MASON SHOULD LIVE BY
The True Meaning of Being a Mason

C. FRED KLEINKNECHT, JR.
33° Past Sovereign Grand Commander

Westphalia Press
An Imprint of the Policy Studies Organization
Washington, DC
2017

Westphalia Press
An imprint of Policy Studies Organization
1527 New Hampshire Ave., NW
Washington, D.C. 20036
info@ipsonet.org

ISBN-10: 1-63391-581-6
ISBN-13: 978-1-63391-581-7

Cover and interior design by Jeffrey Barnes
jbarnesbook.design

Daniel Gutierrez-Sandoval, Executive Director
PSO and Westphalia Press

Updated material and comments on this edition
can be found at the Westphalia Press website:
www.westphaliapress.org

To the memory of a Great Man!

These principles are what all Freemasons should live by, they are the true meaning of Freemasonry. This book will not only benefit the Freemason but everyone can profit. I pass this along to you as a record of the Kleinknecht legacy of leadership. It is offered in hope and belief that it will inspire all who read it today as it has inspired countless others in the past—especially those of us fortunate enough to have been personally blessed by Fred's friendship as well as his wisdom. Fred was the "true" meaning of a Mason and all masons of today would be better people and Masons if they would follow and live by these 33 principles.

I found this book recently on the top of a shelf of our Florida beach house. What a treasure! After reading through it carefully, I thought it necessary to publish. The true meaning of Masonry has gone astray and it needs to come back desperately. This would be a great book for the new mason and for the old that has lost his way.

Mrs. Gene Kleinknecht

(2/21/1926 to 6/22/2017)

CONTENTS

FOREWORD

In my opinion, far too many Americans in our country have sunk to a level of shame and lack of moral and ethical standards from which it will be hard to overcome. There are signs that people may be tiring of this present condition. One can only hope help is on the way.

Perhaps it is!

A voice stilled by death is once again speaking to us, not only in vocal words but also the written word. Found among other papers was a manuscript written by Fred Kleinknecht prior to his death. Retrieved by his wife, now available for print.

Correctly diagnosing the negatives and pitfalls of today's society, Fred has given us his insight into the correct way of life many of us crave. Outstanding advice to the Mason and our proper role in society we are given a pathway to that old Masonic cliché "we make good men better."

Fred Kleinknecht in his book shares his thoughts on the basic "do's" and "don'ts" for a successful life and a vastly better society. This small book should not just be read—it should be studied!

Richard E. Fletcher, PGM (VT)

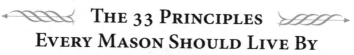

THE 33 PRINCIPLES
EVERY MASON SHOULD LIVE BY
The True Meaning of Being a Mason

by C. Fred Kleinknecht, Jr.
33° Past Sovereign Grand Commander

It's not that the survival of Masonry lies in trying new things. Instead, it lies in excitement, in men being passionate about their Fraternity, about men from every walk of life bringing their talents, and their creativity to Freemasonry. It is a talent, excitement, and creativity that constantly renew our fraternity—assuring its survival.

No one ever said that being a Mason is easy. It is a constant challenge to commit to building bridges rather than walls. Perhaps hardest of all, it requires that we give to others the same freedoms we demand of ourselves.

Masonry started as something like a labor union or trade association, changed into a society of men who enjoyed spending time together discussing the new arts and sciences, changed again by adding mutual aid and assistance and changed again by adding ritual, moral awareness, and public philanthropy.

The thirst for knowledge—what in the Craft we call "Light"—is as real in man as thirst to drink. To quench this thirst for understanding, the Scottish Rite offers a flow of knowledge, bound by the riverbanks of tradition, that is endless.

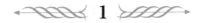

Values

The Blue Lodge ritual teaches that it is the inward and not the outward qualities of a man which matter. Honesty, honor, integrity, compassion, and, all the other virtues, ancient in human experience continue into the future, at least as goals, so long as we aspire to them.

There is a center in society, just as there is in a battle line, and there is also a center in each individual. This societal and individual center consists of shared values and ideals. If the center in any of these is lost, disaster follows.

We have only to look around us to see the results when these values weaken. As barriers of decency fall like dominoes, the public responds less and less to traditional values. Incidents of violence and aberrant sexuality become more frequent and, in the absence of shame, their depiction is more explicit. Language sinks to the vulgar, then the obscene.

If the moral and ethical center of society and the individual had held, there would be no terrorist bombings, no street gangs, no children hungry or abandoned, no ethnic groups crying unheard for justice, and no demagogues firmly in power. But the daily newspaper and television news offer abundant proof that the center is failing. And if reinforcements do not arrive quickly, the center—and the battle—will be lost.

While the great human truths do not change from age to age and from nation to nation, the non-expression of those truths does change. In particular, it is a tragically clear civilization's center—our ethical values and moral sense lag far behind our technical knowledge.

People make decisions every day based on their values. Each day, every one of us decides to be tolerant or fanatical, compassionate or cold, greedy or sharing, supportive or destructive, curious or ignorant, thoughtful or thoughtless, and loving or distant. In an individual, the sum total of those daily decisions is his character; in a nation, it is its culture. The Scottish Rite affects these decisions and points to the right ones. That is our mission.

We are the teachers and preservers of those personal and societal values to which men must, in time, return if they are to survive. We must bring order from chaos. We must hold the center. At a time when there seems to be more and more debate over a lack of values and personal responsibility in our society, we need to anchor this generation, and all those who follow, to those things we have in common.

Since the time of the early Greeks, societies have used initiation as a way of helping to transform a person into something new and better. Our Masonic leaders have to find imaginative ways to make our Craft relevant and available to young men eager to embrace the values Freemasonry has always brought to the world—family, patriotism, self-improvement, character building, and service to humanity. For the Mason, the common good takes precedence over selfish gain, and the Golden Rule is the standard of personal and public conduct. Actions speak louder than words. Example is a truer test of value than rhetoric.

The laws of existence, though covered by the debris of daily living, are simple and immutable. They wait only for us to discover them through our individual awareness. Then, suddenly, the pieces of the puzzle fall in place and reveal

3

the once fragmented design in its entire, intact oneness and beauty.

The caliber of a person determines his ego, and usually the bigger the ego, the lower the caliber.

Thinking "outside the box" expands possibilities, rather than discarding them. The essentials have not changed. Research surveys tell us that men still want to associate with men of high purpose and standards. Men are still willing, in fact eager, to spend quality time with other men. Men still want to make things better for themselves, their families, and their communities. Men still search for sound moral values, still have a sense that bread alone is not enough, still reach a point in their lives when they have achieved financial or social success, and look around and say, "there has to be something more to life." And the Scottish Rite still has many of the answers they are seeking.

We are the teachers and preservers of those personal and societal values to which men must, in time, return if they are to survive. We must bring order from chaos. We must hold the center.

2

Truth/Wisdom/Integrity/Loyalty

Truth is more important than convenience. What is honorable is more important than what is easy. Knowledge is better than ignorance. Compassion is better than selfishness. For Freemasons, these are more than mottoes or empty aphorisms; they are the conscious decisions that guide our actions and inform our lives.

Our forefathers in Masonry bequeathed deep roots to us, roots which tap the profound wellsprings of faith and honor and dignity and intellectual integrity. These roots connect us in our daily lives to faith traditions. Our Masonic forefathers also bequeathed us wings, ideals that inspire the human spirit to soar above routine of daily life and seek the great Light of Truth.

Freemasonry does not define truth or dictate it. Our fraternity only encourages each person to seek truth for himself. Together, as individuals and Brethren, we are moving forward and leaving any fortress-minded antagonist to fend for himself while we seek, in brotherhood, the good that benefits all.

Wisdom is developed only when you have looked at the information, thoughtfully evaluated it, applied your own ethical and moral standards, leavened it with humility, and seasoned it with perspective.

As with all thoughtful men, Masonry has helped me realize my shortcomings as well as my strengths. It has helped me to become a better person.

Integrity matters. Is there one of us who does not value the friends who do what they say they will do, or who can be counted on to be entirely fair in everything? Is there one of us who does not wish to be such a person?

Honesty is an essential component of integrity. We admire the men or women who tell the truth, no matter what. And we still distrust people we have caught in a lie.

Are integrity and other values our Order teaches still pertinent to humankind? The answer to each of these questions depends on the world you wish to leave for your children and grandchildren.

One of the great lessons of the Rite is this: we do not inherit the world, we create it. We shape our fate—and the world— by the choices we make, the actions we take, and the way we decide to live our lives.

The fundamental loyalty of Mason to Mason has always been our greatest strength. It preserved our fraternity in the dark days of the Masonic oppressions in our first century, and through the trials and challenges of the second. Times without number, it has been the factor which allowed individual members of the Fraternity to live through days of despair and sorrow as during World War II and the fascist suppression of the Craft throughout Europe. Now, in our third century, it is every bit as important as ever.

Loyalty has made possible the great truth that Masons never meet as strangers. Required even at the risk of life, loyalty is the bedrock without which Masonry simply could not exist.

As the modern world tears at us with stresses and demands; as we find ourselves more and more caught up in an age which values the quick, the cheap, and the superficial, where acquaintanceship must suffice for most men and honest friendship becomes rare; let us never lose sight of loyalty.

3

Tradition

The same basic physical, social, religious, and spiritual needs which motivated the ancient Egyptian on the banks of the Nile motivate the Masonic Brother today. The expression of those needs may have changed, along with the ways in which we try to meet them—but the needs, basic to humanity, have not.

Sometimes non-Mason friends tell us that Masonry isn't the real world. But it IS the real world; the rest is substitute. In culture that has substitutes for everything including ideals, Masonry provides a healthy dose of reality.

Masonry teaches real ethics and morality, based on the real experience of generations over centuries. It insists men and women have real obligations to each other as children of God. It advances real integrity as the cornerstone of a truly successful life. It provides the moral compass, the values, and lessons, to guide us through these days of crisis.

Masonic unity begins in the heart of the individual Mason. It comes from a deep knowledge that Masonry is good and does good. It comes from a deep commitment to Masonry prospering as a whole and to making that happen. It comes from a personal involvement in the Unity. It means that you talk up, not down, to every Masonic Body, whether you are active in it or not. We are a family. We support each other unconditionally.

Masonry is bigger and greater than any man. It is not a monument to an individual, but to an ideal. It is not the fiefdom of a particular office, but a field of common effort and work. It is not the private feast of a ruler, but the common banquet in which all share as equals.

Masonry works, and works well, as long as we all work, as long as every Mason cares more about the task than the glory, more about the outcome than the credit, and more about doing something than being someone.

 **4**

Tolerance

For all of us, tolerance of others always faces danger from the darker side of human nature. It is easy to be tolerant of someone who agrees with us, whose situation and life experience are similar to our own. It is less easy to be tolerant of someone with beliefs we personally consider wrong.

No one should be "persuaded" of any religious truth by use of the rack or the stake, or by threat of political, social, or economic persecution, or by war or any means by which men have bullied others against their will.

We hold dear some truths which have been out of favor in the last few decades—truths about honor and integrity and the moral nature of man, and human decency, and intellectual, religious, political, and economic freedom. Without genuine tolerance of others, those beliefs ring false.

Masonry concerns itself with the practical problems of living, and one cannot live well if one is intolerant, careless of the thoughts and feelings of others, or mean spirited and unforgiving.

The great lessons of the dignity of each individual, the vital importance of toleration, and the right to spiritual, political, and intellectual liberty—these values are as relevant today as they have ever been in the past.

5

Philanthropy/Charity

5000 Members for the Scottish Rite Research Society

Every Mason abides by the "Golden Rule," however it is stated, and labors in all aspects of his life to fulfill Freemasonry's goals of charity in both senses of the word— philanthropy to those in need and loving brotherhood for all mankind.

Giving of ourselves in small ways will build a positive habit so that we can go on to offer assistance in larger matters. Each of us has real talent and ability. Yes, our time is precious and we have many obligations that must be met. But take the time to lend a hand, and you will be amazed at the results.

Our contributions to life today will endure when we are long gone from the mortal scene, but the spirit in which we made that contribution will live forever. Give to this world your best, for in doing so you prepare yourself for the best in the world to come.

A selfish person will never be the servant to all. It is to be the servant of all that we have accepted our task and responsibility.

The media may lionize examples of wealth and conspicuous consumption, yet in our hearts we admire the great men and women of deep roots and strong wings who sacrifice themselves and work to make the lives of others better.

One of the great missions of our Order is philanthropy.

Charity is the final greatest guide to our actions. We so often think of charity only as giving of ourselves. Its fullest meaning is love in all its forms. One of those forms is a child-like generosity, a delight in being helpful for its own sake. Masons have learned that the warm feeling of doing good is all the reward any of us should ever need.

If we believe in charity, let us find new opportunities to be more charitable—remembering that charity is not just a matter of giving money. Let us look for opportunities to invest our time, our care, and our compassion as well as our dollars.

Charity is an attitude, a mind-set, a value system that has at its roots the profound conviction: *people matter more than things.*

Freemasonry is not only compatible with religion but also confirms and complements religious faith and church, synagogue, or mosque participation. The principles of our Fraternity are based on the same moral absolutes that form the foundation of all true faith. Every Mason must believe in a Supreme Being. He must strive to live morally of individual character and social conduct.

6

Fraternity

What does it mean to be fraternal, to treat a Brother as a Brother? It means we take the time and trouble to care. It means we are at least as concerned about his welfare as we are of our own. A selfish Mason is a contradiction in terms.

Fraternalism is truly the April shower of Masonry. It brings forth growth and new life to us all as well as to those who we serve. It is a quiet pleasure to stand for a moment in the purifying, nourishing rain.

Because human nature has not changed since our Fraternity began, our teachings must continue to convey and expound the timeless moral and philosophical truths intended to improve the quality of life for all humankind. Bringing Light to the world is the goal of every true Freemason.

But without the special care we give each other through fraternalism, there is little point in whatever else we may do. We may fund great charitable enterprises, but if we fail to treat each other as Brothers, our charity is hollow. We may study the great philosophies of the ages as represented in our ritual, but if we fail the test of friendship, we have done little.

No building, no matter how magnificent, is as permanent and powerful as an act of fraternalism. With determination, we can make fraternalism—and the Scottish Rite—grow in every nook and cranny.

The pleasure we get in associating with Masonic Brothers,

the confidence we have that we can trust these men under any circumstances—these fundamentals are vital in a world which seems to grow more selfish and less loving every day.

7

Cheer

Biennial Session Dinner with Ernest Borgnine

The paradox of happiness is that it comes from selflessness. To enjoy it ourselves, we must bring it to others. To be selfish and mercenary is to be miserable, but to give without thought of return is to be happy. There is a deep, lasting happiness, a soul satisfaction beyond the reach of the senses, in sharing with others. Prove it with a smile or gracious comment. Say thank you. Give overdue congratulations.

Even on a humble, daily level, thinking of others is a potent force for change. It creates a new mood, a lighter atmosphere, opens new avenues of communication. The person who seemed distant and cool often becomes cordial and warm—all at no more cost than a cheerful smile or handshake.

Few people realize that real happiness is so inexpensive. In truth, it costs nothing. Its currency is caring. Investments are not made in dollars but in acts of kindness and concern.

Conversely, money, status, and power are counterfeits of true happiness, and how we pay dearly for them.

In the classic Greek drama *Oedipus* the chorus admonishes, "Call no man happy until he is dead." By contrast, the upbeat lyrics of a modern song lightly describe life as "just a bowl of cherries." For most of us, the truth lies somewhere in the middle, a complex mixture that differs from day to day or moment to moment. But deliberate cheer changes that balance for the better.

There is a good motto which states: "If you see someone without a smile, give him yours." Good cheer is infectious. Others will respond to a warm greeting, a true sense of friendliness. It requires a mindset and attitude that sees the good despite the petty flaws, however annoying.

Cheer creates cheer, just as the laughter of one person in an audience is caught and echoed by another until everyone shares in the lightness of spirit. Humor halves any burden and reveals possibilities that a dark temper would be sure to overlook. And part of good cheer is the willingness to help. This need not be a saint-like altruism though such total self-sacrifice is much to be admired.

Each person chooses his attitude, his "cheer." He can choose, if he wishes, hope over despair, courage over fear, love over hatred, joy over melancholy, trust over suspicion, faith over doubt, and compassion over contempt.

Contrary to the false promises of modern advertising, happiness is neither purchased nor obtained through material acquisition. Contentment, happiness, and serenity lie solely with the confines of the human breast, or they are not found at all.

8

Education

Since the founding of the Craft, Masons have been champions of public education, social justice, thoughtful patriotism, and religious toleration.

We support excellence in public education with treatment for learning problems, with financial assistance, and with moral leadership that refuses to compromise with barbarism or mediocrity.

The Nation's educational system could become narrow enclaves, divided by race, sex, politics, class, ethnic origin, religion, and scholastic ability. If society is so divided, part of the common identity that people share as Americans would be lost.

By initiation, by progressive learning, and by understanding, we leave ignorance and move toward the light of knowledge.

The combination of learning and giving is a powerful symbol of a successful life. Learning and giving keep us spiritually young and vital.

It may be fashionable with some people to attack and vilify our public schools today and blame them for all of society's ills, but we Masons will not join that chorus. We believe the public schools and the people who labor in them deserve our support, not unfair criticism. We are dedicated to resisting any assault by sectarian interests on the ability of the public school system to serve all students of all creeds.

9

Family/Youth

Barbara Bush

The family is at the center of everything spiritual, emotional, and even economic. Nurturing the family and the conditions which surround it should be the first concern of every government, every public organization, and every private institution.

Birth is swift when compared with years of support, reinforcement, and help a child or family needs to grow, gain strength, and mature. A family has to be fed with tears of the spirit. It takes a true emotional investment to make a family work—not just by parents, though their expenditure should be the greatest.

The Scottish Rite can help, not so much as an institution but as individual Masons armed with the teachings we have learned and the disciplines of self-development. We cannot make the mind, heart, and soul of a family, but we can help to keep a family whole. We provide information about what makes families successful. We host events for the fam-

18

ily. We supply nurturing fun and fellowship in wholesome surroundings. We counter the conditions of poverty, ignorance, loneliness, and drug dependence that crush both the family and the child. We help find ways to remove roadblocks to success.

It is far better to be bound to life than be shackled to death. To commit to the family and its values is to choose life. It gives us purpose and challenge. It raises us beyond the limits of our personal zone of comfort and into the greater world outside ourselves.

There may be no aspect of life in which equilibrium is more important. Parents who have little time for their children should not be surprised if their children have little time for them. Such things as love, trust, confidence, and morality are learned and not developed. If we weigh down one side of the balance with indifference, hostility, suspicion, anger, or unreasonable demands, we should not be surprised when the other side of the balance flies away from the center line. And "family values" include "values taught in the family." As we build our families and our own values, we build our world.

Only by strengthening the family as the source and transmitter of values can we assure safe, secure, and happy lives.

Family is central to our civilization. It is the source of security, the place where values are shared and transmitted to the young. It is the place of refuge. It is the source of our worthiest hopes.

Progress is possible only because each generation learns what past generations knew and discovered. When a family functions as a family, when it is the place in which values are passed from generation to generation, those values give a strength nothing can break.

Unfortunately, the lures of valueless living have produced a chasm between many parents and their children. There is a spiritual emptiness in some Americans, and this leads to false "families," such as street gangs and religious cults, and many other forms of extremism. There is no cure for these ills that can be mandated by government or imposed by social workers. Only by strengthening the American family and by reinforcing its ancient role as the source and transmitter of values, can we assure safe streets and secure lives?

Strong family values balance the needs of husband, wife, and children. When marriage is strong, the children will benefit immeasurably. When the marriage fails, the children will be torn between parents, disoriented, and desolated by being forced to make a choice between the two people in the world who mean the most to them.

There is a world of difference between a house and a home. A house is a building of mortar and stone but a home is "the abiding-place of ardent affection, of fervent hope, of genial trust." The future values of life, if not learned in the home, many never be learned anywhere else. Save the home and family and you save civilizations.

Youth

To Fred Kleinknecht
With best wishes,
G Bush

President George Bush, Sr.

A sturdy tree or a beautiful flower can only come from a good seed, but in reaching its full potential it depends on the influence of things outside itself; good soil, enough water, and warm temperature. The same is true of children. They need the nurture of reliable physical and emotional support, and unfailing love.

Scottish Rite Freemasons dream of the day when every child has a full command of communication skills, written, and spoken, and each child will be able to develop the gifts, the talents given him or her by God. To reach that day will require our gifts of money, talent, and time. No facet of Scottish Rite growth in the last decade has been more heartwarming and fulfilling than the increase and improvement in our network of clinics, centers, and programs assisting children with learning disorders. There is no better way to say "Thank you" for the gifts we ourselves have received from the Creator than to share the gift of learning to others. There is no more noble work than to give a child a brighter future and, at the same time, guarantee our nation a better tomorrow.

How do you put a price on providing a child with the ability to walk and run and play again, to overcome language problems, and to be able to lead a normal life? How do you assign a dollar value to hope, or tears of gratitude, or comfort in time of sorrow and lost? The children of the world are Masonry's bottom line. And it's the bottom line that counts.

We don't usually hear about the millions of good, productive young people who contribute to the wellbeing of this nation. They work hard and follow the rules. They go to school, labor at decent jobs, help around the home, obey their parents, and belong to school groups that assist their community. Instead of telling us about those who take off and land safely, our media thrive on stories of the young people who crash and burn—in gangs, on drugs—and hurt others.

Whether with our own children, or with the youth of the community, masons can serve as role models of the values America cherishes. We can inspire the young with our lives, as thousands of generations of fathers have done before us.

What more precious gift can one give than hope to those who follow us? Without hope, all appears lost. With it, there is a ray of light in even the darkest night.

To a child, however, hope is a bright bird, which once flown, surely will never return. A child's grief over a broken toy, lost friend, or missed pleasure is all the keener because childhood's horizons are close. All is now. The past, even yesterday, is long forgotten and tomorrow is a distant abstraction.

As adults and parents, we see the longer perspective. By offering endless amounts of love, we can bring stability and hope in the place of chaos and despair. It is the child who is left to his own devices, who feels abandoned and unloved, not the child who is counseled and guided by his parents.

We learn, children included, by seeing and doing. If children see you act rightly, they will learn the principle and the fact of right action. Unfortunately, the opposite is also true. Act on whim, against what is correct and with animosity rather than generosity, and your children will learn accordingly. Bad seed grows as strongly as good, and the harvest is bitter.

When parental control is misguided or oppressive, it can stunt and distort.

First, love abundantly. That is easy to say, but not always so easy to do. Too often we let life's problems harry us. We become absorbed in things and forget that people are what is really important in life. Our children are our lives in that they will carry our beliefs and what we have taught them into the future. If our message to tomorrow is to do well and benefit others, it must be positive, encompassing, and strong.

Loving is never easy, but in its simple, insistent offer of self it is an unfailing bond between parent and child, a silver cord that is stronger than death.

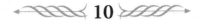

10

Reverence

Often misunderstood, trivialized or simply lost in the fast-moving world of declining values is a word that seems old-fashioned today, but is still what Freemasonry and life are all about: Reverence. In this one sense, our brotherhood may be said to be R-rated.

When we have reverence for ourselves, we do not pollute our bodies, our minds, or our souls. We have reverence for our parents and forebears who have given us our lives and this great country. We have reverence for others and advocate every measure that will uplift and benefit humankind. We have reverence for the Creator and demonstrate this fact by supporting our places of worship and conforming to our actions to the Volume of Sacred Law or our religion.

Sadly reverence is a declining virtue in the world today. Without it we transgress the laws of God and man. Without it we shatter the unwritten ordinances that govern the universe and form the basis of our craft. To abuse one's body with alcohol and drugs, to defile one's mind with pornography, to contradict via violence the moral insight given to us by our Creator—these are not acts of reverence for life, but acts of destruction. Reverence has no special time or place of its own. Its hour is now and always. By being properly reverent today, this very hour, we reveal our likeness to God and create a better, happier, wiser world.

Growth

Growth of all sorts—in fraternal knowledge and personal understanding, in friends and fellowship for each member and his family, and in opportunities to serve one's fellow men—is one of the primary benefits of the Scottish Rite. Today, with Freemasonry under attack for its history of religious toleration, church/state separation, and advocacy of education, there is strength in knowing and appreciating our order's deep-rooted heritage of personal development.

Freemasonry makes good men better—better husbands and fathers, better workers and teachers, as well as better citizens and church members. Our fraternity does not compete. It enhances and encourages each Brother's participation in the groups or activities of his choice. Freemasonry is an elixir of youth, of energy, of personal fulfillment.

Masons go beyond narrow sectarianism and limiting dogma. The mission of Freemasonry is to bring the best from faulted existence and human nature—to take a rough stone and make it into a perfect ashlar. In Freemasonry itself, we see a force that truly brings out the "angel within" by positively affecting every aspect of life from individual self-improvement to the building of a happier, wiser, and better world for all humankind.

If we are to experience Masonic growth and rediscovery, we must sail into waters unknown to us—into new community involvement, Masonic education, and a compassionate commitment to others.

As Masons, our actions speak louder than any words. Our best references are our tolerance of others, our acceptance of all good men, and our support of worthy civic and philanthropic efforts, such as our nationwide network of Scottish Rite Childhood Language Disorders Centers.

Our rate of personal growth is always a function or our willingness to change. We get out of Freemasonry what we put in. The mason who cares—who gets involved, who attends Lodge and Temple, and who forms the iron link of Masonry's mystic tie with his Craft Brother—experiences such growth. Freemasonry is a way of life that enriches each member everywhere in every way. His home and office, his work and his leisure, as well as his church and service club all benefit through personal growth in the rich soil of Freemasonry's universal truths.

Freemasonry's roots are deep, strong, and branch widely to all aspects of endeavor. Our Craft transcends time. It reaches from the dim past to today's headlines. It embraces all. It includes good men everywhere regardless of language, race, or geographical location. It inspires right action from universal principles. Masonry has a rich past, yes, but its present is as great.

In becoming a Freemason, a good man becomes better. He joins himself to a tradition of excellence that spans all human history. He enters as an equal in a Fraternity where merit and service are the only criteria of acceptance. He multiples the effectiveness of the good he can do by joining his effort to the united strength of millions.

Putting the prestige, pride, and fellowship of being a Mason aside, there is one central reason for becoming a Mason— to be able to do more good than any individual could possibly do by himself and, in achieving this good, to grow in intellect, in morality, and in spirit.

Character

There are those who would cheapen human life and human values by telling us that we are only a bundle of reflexes and nerves. They say that we choose what we are led to choose by instincts and desires for which we are not responsible. Theories of this kind degrade humanity and make man nothing more than a high order of animal. The ultimate conclusion of such theories is one of pessimistic failure.

Others would explain us away on the basis of how much we possess or how well we are known by the public.

It is not fate or chemistry that makes us who we are. It is not possessions or reputation.

The course of our lives and our ultimate value to others is determined by one thing above all else: our character.

The people respected most by people we, in turn, can respect are not those who blame their flaws and failures on bad luck or faulty wiring, nor are they the boastful, hollow heroes and heroines manufactured by press agents and tabloid hype. Instead, they are those people who care and sacrifice for others. They would rather help a child, assist a worthy cause, or contribute their time to a community project than simply add another check to their bank account or garner a line on the society page. Their most basic common denominator is character.

Each of us is bound to his Brother by fraternal feeling and common idealism. Nothing moves the soul as strongly as idealism, and idealism lies at the heart of character. Freemasonry offers a system of philosophy that combines within itself the best insights of the best minds—and the strongest characters—from ancient times to the modern era.

# 13

Ritual

Ritual gives us a sense of connectedness with our past, our family, our friends, our nation, and our faith. It is a series of learning and transforming experiences through which we become what we are. Reality and ritual are not opposites or antagonists. They are closely related as the oak and acorn.

Ritual opens our hearts to our society's great lessons. Properly performed, it moves our souls and reveals to each of us our spiritual and physical potential.

The whole structure of Freemasonry is based on the ritual-rich Symbolic Lodge. It is here that good men learn the ideals of our Order. Here they catch the fervor of Freemasonry. Here they learn from their Brethren just what it is to be a Mason. Masonic labor enriches in ways well beyond monetary return. It fulfills the spirit. It reveals new possibilities. It nurtures the ties of brotherhood and belonging. Ritual serves that process of renewal.

Our principles of brotherhood, relief, truth, justice, and freedom are fundamental to all societies at all times. They offer tangible benefits and absolute values. They liberate the human spirit and succor our human needs.

Men need to retreat from the world from time to time, to refresh and recharge their spiritual and emotional batteries. The Lodge provides that safe place protected by custom and strengthened by ritual. No soldier can withstand the pressure of conflict without a break. And no place of refuge is as secure as that constructed by men who understand the need for values and shared commitment.

The goal of the Scottish Rite is understanding, not data; wisdom, not information. The Symbolic Lodge is the core of our Craft. It is the foundation upon which all else in Freemasonry depends. The basic, universal, and eternal lessons of the three degrees form the sound foundation upon which we build our lives. In our lodge, we learn to become Masons in our hearts. No degree is more important than the other, for the principles of the Lodge bring us integrity and strong character, dignity, and respect. In return, we strive to be of service to others through our charitable endeavors and our steadfast concern for individual liberty and freedom.

Our Craft, as a refuge for men of integrity and as a command post for those who wish to advance human progress, remains strong and intact. Our values will still be here to serve the world after any storm has passed.

14

Leadership

President Ronald Reagan

The first responsibly of any leader is to secure the future of his organization, whether that is a nation, a business, or a fraternity.

Leadership is not a matter of youth or age; it is a matter of determination. It is not dependent on having a title or an official position. It depends on personal dedication, commitment, and character.

Properly respectful of tradition, we too often put dedicated conservators into positions of leadership instead of dynamic innovators. The conservators are more intent on not "rocking the boat" than in charting new ways to Masonic accomplishment.

Sometimes, we pick leaders as a misguided way of honoring long service. When longevity is the primary criterion, uncertain leadership results. Capable younger candidates lose their enthusiasm to contribute because their talents are not appreciated and employed.

A nation, an army, an institution, a company, a committee, and a family—without leadership each lacks direction and power. Although the human resources may exist, they cannot be tapped, and the result is stagnation. In any group, large or small, valid, dynamic and personal leadership must come to the fore and inspire voluntary cooperation. True success entails a sense of personal involvement and fulfillment on the part of all members, not just the satisfaction of the leader.

To achieve this, a leader must have charisma that almost magical ability to motivate and then guide without the slightest hint or appearance of coercion. Charisma comes from the Greek term meaning "divine gift." The charismatic leader touches on elemental truths, on principles innate in the spiritual structure of the universe. In expressing these truths, he strikes a mutual chord in the hearts and minds of his fellow men, for they too, have these essential ideals embedded in their souls. Thus, in supporting the leader, each individual also follows the dictates of his own mind and heart. The leader's will is not tyrannical but becomes the focal point of each individual's personal intuition of what is right and just.

Leadership is not the result of meeting current fashions, nor can it be created by image-managers. Leadership that works is always based on character.

Each of us, to one degree or another, is a gem in the rough. We all have our sharp edges and human foibles. We come to the door of Freemasonry as imperfect men, rough ashlars to be squared and polished by the teachings of our Fraternity. The leader builds with rough and smooth alike and he overlooks the petty faults of human nature.

The leader blends the best qualities of every Brother into a concerted effort that benefits the Fraternity as a whole. He works with people, not around them or against them, for he knows that "people power" is the source of Masonry's impact on the world.

The true leader, the one fully deserving of his rank and honors, remains fully responsive to the Brethren he leads.

In any great mission, there is no room for personal vanity. The goal of the institution, its ideal, is the essential thing. Consequently, the leader does not have to worry about his personal prestige, his dignity.

The man who claims the accomplishments of others more often appears a fool than a wise man. By giving credit where it is deserved, the leader rightly recognizes merit and, at the same time, inspires continued effort.

A leader is best when people barely know he exists. He talks little. He seeks no acclaim. He does not command, but inspires. And when his work is done, his aim fulfilled, those he has led do not herald his accomplishment.

Rather, they say, "We did it ourselves."

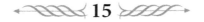

Success

W e are limited only by the number of events and community services we decide to do. Only apathy and laziness can keep us from success.

Life shrinks or expands in proportion to one's courage, and Freemasonry can inspire each Brother with the moral fiber and personal commitment so essential to success. Success, after all, is failure turned inside out.

Individual success depends on finding the right work, toiling on unaware that the best part of life is passing them by. They are easily discouraged and let the opinions of others weigh them down. The successful man looks to himself, not others. He is an individual, free, and self-reliant. What matters is his opinion, his knowledge, not the attitudes of others.

That is not to say that others play no role in any successful person's life. One individual may brag about being "self-made." Another may claim that "nobody helped me." But neither boast is likely to be true. The successful person, if he or she is really honest, will think of good teachers or friends who helped at critical moments.

We do not know what we can accomplish until we try. I once knew a young man who was depressed because he was failing nearly all his classes. I asked him if he was really trying. He admitted he wasn't. "Then you haven't failed," I said. "You just haven't tried." Realizing this, his spirits lifted. With his new perspective, he stopped thinking of himself as a loser and his frame of mind changed. He was soon really trying and really succeeding.

Success is more than simple ability. It depends more on how we use our native talents. Gold unmined is worthless. Yet every man of character has gold inside him in the forms of courage, determination, and creativity.

Look at the origin of the word "work." It means "action" and "tool." You must do more than think about success. You must take action to accomplish it and use the tools given to you by the Creator. Like Edison's definition of genius, success is more perspiration than inspiration.

Becoming discouraged helps no one, least of all the person who is discouraged. Have you ever seen any result from apathy and despair than more apathy and despair? Do not let others extinguish your flame. Keep it burning—not matter what the circumstances, no matter what others say. High aspiration feeds itself. It also breeds success.

The idea that we can't succeed assures we don't succeed. And the converse is true as well—try and you will succeed. No one holds you back but yourself. The questions are: Is there work? Are you able? Can you succeed?

Courage

Edwin "Buzz" Aldrin, leaving the House of the Temple

Blessed are the heroes and heroines who risk their lives, their fortunes, their futures, their reputations, or their chances for advancement for some vision of a greater cause. Without them, we would still be crouching in caves, fearing the night. Great heroes are always risk-takers.

Heroes prove the impossible can come true when the right cause is in harmony with the right resolve. Every generation has it heroes. They bring identity to the collective consciousness. Every nation is blessed because of its heroes. Men and women, in our time, have made us today better than what we were yesterday.

That is the importance of heroes and of heroism. Our heroes are the untold legions of human beings who give up a part of themselves and of their own self-interest for no other reason than that they wish to serve. Because of them, our lives are richer and better. They are the real heroes of our time and every time.

We do not always know their names, and often we are unaware of their deeds. But we live better, richer, and longer lives because of them.

Heroism isn't a goal but a consequence. The person who sets out to be a hero will fail, because he or she is setting out not to serve others, but to gratify their own ego. That produces a bore, but it never produces a hero. Heroism isn't a matter of convenience, it's an irresistible impulse. The hero doesn't help others when he has nothing better to do; he does it because it doesn't occur to him not to do it.

Heroes are not mass produced, nor instantly available. Each is unique, each is handcrafted.

Heroism happens when men or women decide that they personally are less important than the job to be done, the cause to be defended, or the wrong to be righted. Most heroic men and women had no intention of being heroes or heroines. They simply did what needed to be done and, in the process, changed part of the world. Sometimes, they gave their lives in an attempt to save others. Their determination, dedication, and often their stubbornness made the difference.

These are some of the reasons the majority of people do not choose heroism. Most of us would rather bemoan the injustices of life than strive to correct them. We would rather fume about the oppressions of big government than become politically active and work to correct those wrongs. We would rather lament that children of today are not receiving a quality education than get elected to the school board and fight to improve education in our area.

Like Hamlet, we would rather bear those ills we know than fly to others that we know not.

Physical courage, heroism, or bravery under enemy fire must have a moral underpinning. They require a commitment within the person's innermost being that the cause in which he is engaged is a just one, worth fighting for and, if necessary, dying for. It takes great souls and strong men to face bayonet and shrapnel despite their fears. The greatness of man is unfolded in the crisis experiences of life.

No battle, no war has settled forever the issues of life that matter in the hearts of a free people. There is always the dream of a world free from hate, where every mortal has a chance; a world free from the tyrant's heel, where all men can be free; a peaceful world with opportunity for all to pursue the good life.

Heroes are made of the same varied mix of doubt and faith, fear and courage, as well as lethargy and energy as any of us—although perhaps in different proportions. What makes them successful is that they accent the positive. They believe if you can't solve a problem one way, find another. They dare to think great thoughts and to live them. If we *will* to be great, we can be great. We can conquer if we believe we can. There are crises every day, opportunists to go the extra mile or slack off, challenges to surmount or push aside, principles to follow or disregard, and kindnesses to perform or leave ungiven.

There is as much courage as in warfare, though less spectacularly demonstrated, in meeting the small challenges of daily living, rearing families, going to work, sharing with those less fortunate, participating in our civic duties, and trying to make this world a little better when we leave it than it was when we entered it.

Each of us can be a grass-roots hero to our family, our business associated, our fellow citizens, and our fraternal

Brethren. All it takes is the courage to follow our higher instincts, and the thirst for what is right, just and compassionate. These are the same principles the Creator made part of His creation and, therefore, part of each of us.

The next time you look in the mirror, see a hero. See yourself as the Creator made you—and as He knows that you can be.

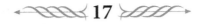

Prayer/Faith

Believe in God!

If there is anything that will give you a great sense of personal power, it is a practical and workable belief in God. As surely as you need water when you are thirsty and food when you are hungry, you need real faith in a personal God.

We never need to fear. The love of God is always there to nourish and support us. However, dead nature may appear in the bleakest of winters, summers abundance is harbored safely beneath the snow. However, desolate our spirit initially may be during the holiday season, or any other time of year, God's eternal and restorative love is forever available for the asking. We call this prayer.

Prayer is psychologically sound. It will help you release the great natural powers you have inside. It will give you a new, inward poise that can and will be translated into everyday results. It is how we ask the Creator for His direction in our lives. And often, it is the means by which He answers our request.

Our first duty as Masons is to act in accordance with what we believe—the great principles of Faith, Hope, and Charity. Prayer is the language of that action.

Faith

To have true faith in ourselves, we must believe both in our ability to perform and in God's guidance of all things. If we are confident that a desired end will come about, we don't worry about when it will happen. We just proceed step-by-step with whatever actions it takes to get there.

We don't waste time or spiritual energy begrudging the success of another who has completed the steps quicker than we have. If we fear we will never achieve our end, however, then we cannot be content when another achieves what we have not.

Faith and reason—the ability to believe and the ability to question—are essential to a healthy spirit.

Just as it is true that faith feeds the spirit and fills the person's life with love and strength, so it is true that the man or woman without faith leads a life of loneliness and emotional poverty. Faith is essential to us if we are to be truly human.

And yet faith without joy is worse than no faith at all. Faith without joy has led to the horrors of the Inquisition, the "pinched-face faith" of the Puritans, and to all forms of intolerance which have cost so much in human suffering. It is no wonder that great thinkers of all religions have stressed the importance of a joyful spirit.

In many ways, fire is like faith, pristine, and powerful, a primal force that can bring gentle guidance, like a candle in a window, or an enormous potential for destruction, like a fanatic's single-minded pursuit of his special beliefs.

Faith is a matter of conviction. So why argue? Masonic tradition is against such a debate. Our non-engagement, some say, leaves the field of victory to others. I say, we have moved the conflict to another field, the arena of actions, not talk.

We are architects of more than mortar and stone, of hospitals, temples, and learning centers. We are architects of faith, builders of better men and nations.

Let us avoid the pessimist's dark way. Let us light our paths and those of others with the guiding candles of our confidence, our hope, our faith. Together, we can light the way for all mankind.

The pilgrim has no fortress to defend. His personal faith is shared with others, to be sure, but not pressed on them by any force other than that of example. Such is Freemasonry. Ours is a pilgrim of faith, not a fortress mentality.

In Freemasonry, no doctrine, no dogma, and no finely drawn lines confine or limit the mission of the human mind and spirit to seek truth, liberty, and the betterment of humankind, both for the individual and for his society. Yet Freemasonry has no theology, no litmus test of right or wrong other than its strong advocacy of toleration. Doctrine and dogma are matters for religions, not fraternities, and each Freemason has his own church or synagogue, or mosque. It is his by birth or choice, and Freemasonry encourages and enhances his support of it, whatever his faith.

Faith and freedom are inextricably intertwined. Where one exists, the other must inevitably follow. To have faith in a Supreme Creator is essential for freedom. That is why today's garrison states espouse atheism. If man abandons faith in Deity, he loses an essential element of faith in himself and becomes a ready victim for oppression.

In many ways, fire is like faith, pristine, and powerful, a primal force that can bring gentle guidance, like a candle in a window, or an enormous potential for destruction, like a fanatic's single-minded pursuit of his special beliefs.

What does a candle lose by lighting others? Rather than diminish its radiance, a candle so used engenders more light, more faith, and more commitment in one's self and others to fulfilling God's law of love on this earth.

Hope

Hope, which is desire mixed with the expectation of success, begets confidence. Envy, in the final analysis, implies a lack of these qualities. If we do not achieve our ends when we think we should, we must look back within ourselves to find the faults that prevent us from reaching our goals. We must identify and eliminate those faults, and then try again.

Someone once said that our successes are no more than evidence that we have learned from our families. It is the failures that prove valuable, for it is from them that knowledge springs—but only if one is honest in the evaluation of that failure. It is by a process of constant refinement that we ultimately gain what we desire.

There is beauty in a star, in that point of light that seems to wink at us, as if sharing a secret joke. It reminds us that there is hope for man as long as we do not take ourselves too seriously. It reminds us of perspective and the importance of balance.

A confrontation with a friend or colleague, a disappointment in our investments, the frustrations of daily living all seem very small compared with the immensity of the universe and those laughing stars, inviting us to share in cosmic good humor. The glory and wonder is that each of us can be such a source of brightness in the lives of others. But first we have to decide to care more about them than about ourselves.

Freedom

What distinguishes man from beast, since the Garden of Eden to the world today, is humankinds ability to make moral decisions, to have the knowledge of good and evil, and to choose good. God made man-free because that is the only condition in which such a choice can be made. Man fulfills his God-given nature only when he decides for freedom.

Freedom, whether our own or that of others, is too precious a gift to be abandoned simply because its cost is high. It is the Creator's greatest gift to man.

American freedom is special, one of a kind. Separation of church and state and the religious liberty it ensures are the cornerstone of all the other freedoms we daily take for granted.

The quest for freedom has been a dream in the hearts and minds of men over the ages. The hand of the oppressor has been the weight on the shoulders of many people in many lands over much of human history. The story of civilization is really the story of man's long struggle to take full possession of God's gift, to be truly free. The great peoples of the Ages have been those not content to live in slavery.

History reveals that freedom has come when there were people who made the quest for freedom of paramount importance in their lives. Over and over, freedom is lost when people are so preoccupied with the attainment of luxuries that they overlook the dangers of taking for granted the freedoms they had.

Time and time again great civilizations have fallen, not from lack of might, but because the people lost their sense of values. The decay of nations has come from within. The downfall of empires has been due in a large measure to the weaknesses of tyrants and the insensitivity of people to the higher ideals of life. The quest for freedom is not a new thing, but it must be an eternal quest, lest freedom once won be lost.

Ours has been the land of opportunity for all those who have come to our shores in search of a better life. Freedom to live their lives in peace and without fear protected by our documents of freedom. We are proud that over the life of our Republic, the powers of government have assured that the quest for freedom for all our people has weathered the onslaught of every foe. We are a Nation of free people but the quest for freedom never ends.

We have never advocated conquest, but we have been in the forefront of every cause that would safeguard and protect our freedoms won with the sword and pen over the decades of our history. We believe that every man's quest for freedom should be honored and that the idea of freedom should be instilled in the minds and hearts of all those who enjoy the blessings of freedom in this great land of ours.

The quest for freedom implies that there must be in the hearts of all who cherish freedom a deep sense of responsibility to protect and preserve our freedom documents.

We must be champions of freedom in our day if it is to survive in the hearts of the people. It is the glory of human life that men can choose the best and in choosing the best we can say to all the world that life is not a "tale told by an idiot, full of sound and fury, signifying nothing."

Men will find within the Rite that life can be a glorious quest, a great crusade, a heroic venture. We believe in the glory of human life and, because we do, we will always be vigilant and militant in our defense of human freedom and the right of all people to achieve the glory ordained for them by their Creator.

Our typically American ideals of "life, liberty and the pursuit of happiness" reflect Freemasonry's tenets of individual improvement. Freedom for self and society, and an ethic of work whose goal is not solely material possessions but the deeper happiness of wedding heart, mind, and soul to attaining high goals while serving others.

20

Patriotism

Tested in the fires of civil strife and world war, the Constitution has proved to be the best plan ever conceived by man to govern a free people. For 200 years, the American people have had the great obligation to make it work. It is a living document that must be interpreted by each new generation. We must measure our current freedoms and responsibilities by its high criteria. We must meet its challenge every day and assure that its ideals remain untarnished and strong.

Through the rights it guarantees, America has thrived. Today, we are the freest, strongest, most prosperous country on earth. And we will remain so if we sustain the resolve expressed by the framers of the Constitution and the courage embodied by generations of Americans since that time in Philadelphia over two centuries ago.

The Constitution is what we make of it. And if we neglect our freedoms and sit by idly while others direct the course of our Nation, we have only ourselves to blame.

When Masonry speaks of patriotism, it is not speaking of a mindless and unthinking devotion to country, or some sort of reflex reaction at the sight of our flag. These are unworthy of thinking men and women. Patriotism involves conscious and deliberate choices, not automatic conditioned responses.

Patriotism is a conscious, thoughtful dedication to the welfare of others, to all the people who comprise the nation. It is the heroism of men and women who are prepared to offer the sacrifice of their own lives that others may enjoy the benefits of liberty. Patriotism, a cardinal virtue of the Mason, is the honor we pay to the past and the hope we express for the future.

Our birthright is not consumption, but production; not useless ease, but useful labor.

It is just as important to remember that the glory of a nation is not only in its battles but also in its administration of justice and the care it takes of all its citizens. Mercy, humanity, and compassion are essentials of true patriotism.

Building a nation is like building a house, after it is built it must be carefully maintained or it begins to fall into ruin. A window breaks, the roof starts to leak, the paint begins to peel. In time, it moves past repair. Then it falls to the ground, and where it was, there is only empty sky.

Everything in America today points to the desperate need to restore core values. We fear rather than love our neighbor. Social trust is crumbling or gone. Civic institutions once deemed effective ways to remedy society's woes and deserving of our support are disrupted by scandals and made ineffective by bureaucracy. Civil debate has disintegrated into hurried insults, negative campaigns, and 30 second television spots. At the same time, there is a deep longing for high, clear, moral standards and leaders who embody them. Where are we to find this brave new world?

In truth, our values, institutions, and leaders have failed us only because we have failed them and ourselves. Any new foundation, any return to a civil and civic society must begin with us, with each person. Too often, however, the individual today is self-absorbed. The nation is in danger of becoming an ever more rapidly disintegrating collection of isolated interests. Glued to our television or computer screens, isolated from any group action or interest, we tend to ignore others and forget that what made this nation great was shared experience and mutual commitment.

To create and restore the core values of America today, we must find and release those same values in ourselves. To reverse America's loss of heart, we ourselves must take heart and find in ourselves the moral responsibility, communal purpose, and personal commitment we desire in others. Our churches, community organizations, and political parties cannot do this for us. But each can be a guide if we seek in each the core values we know are right.

They are the same values that made America great: belief in God as the Creator of us all; patriotic love of and service to the country; the work ethic and the dignity of labor; respect for ones fellowman as for one's self; the value of education and knowledge; liberty of conscience and, with it, religious, political, social, and economic freedom.

Our nation would cease to exist without a common foundation of morals and an allegiance to common principles that govern behavior. To be truly free, our nation must be governed by leaders of character, our industries run by managers and directors of conscience, and at every level our society must be drug-free.

The Declaration of Independence remains a viable and crucial document because of the spirit and commitment of its signers who mutually pledged to each other their lives, their fortunes, and their sacred honor.

It is a paradox of human nature that we must lose something before we value it. For example, those who are ill truly appreciate good health; the beggar really knows the value of money; the blind realize the preciousness of sight. This paradox also applies to love of country. We treasure America most when we are abroad. In fact, I doubt that anyone who has not left our shores can fully realize what America means. Perspective clarifies vision. Absence brings realization.

America has been great, not so much by her might, but by the resources of her spirit found in the hearts of a brave people who know there are some things worth dying for.

People are ready to die because they believe in something great. Our Nation is in real trouble when there is no longer a great cause to demand from us the best we have.

We cannot remain free and prosperous if our young people are enslaved by ignorance or drugs and left unguided by positive example.

Albert Pike was a multidimensional man. His special genius was the ability to infuse his whole life with absolute commitment. He had faith in himself and, as importantly, in America. Love of country motivated him, and freedom was his unswerving guide. In Freemasonry, he found these two powerful forces united with a universal and transcendent philosophy.

The majority of the world's people live without what most Americans take for granted. Where we have adequate food and shelter, they have poor nutrition, even famine, and home can be a shanty or a cave. Where Americans have freedom of expression and lives lived in liberty, many peoples across the globe bear the heavy weight of tyranny and endure lives governed by fear and repression.

Too often we clutter our lives to the extent that we see only the surface and not the spirit within. The true meaning of

Christmas, for example, is often lost in a concern for giving the appropriate gift or having a snowfall on that special day. The Easter message of spiritual symbols of physical renewal is long in—eggs, chicks, bunnies, and lilies. On the fourth of July, our sense of what our nations birthday is all about seems to get lost amid the bunting, flags, fireworks, and iced watermelons.

Being an American is more than patriotic fervor, colorful parades, and airy thoughts of human possibilities. Just as our Founding Fathers balanced high ideals with harsh realities in writing the Constitution, so must be both idealistic and practical. This means speaking out for our American freedoms. It also means doing something about them.

As Americans and Freemasons, we share a double glory and duty. Sons of this soil, we are indebted to America for its bounty and opportunity. Brothers in Freemasonry, we are America's staunchest supporters since our Nation comes closest in the history of mankind to fulfilling our Craft's ideal vision of Brotherhood of Man under the Fatherhood of God.

21

Dreams/Ideals

M en have to dream. Without dreams no great inventions are conceived, no great works of art created, and no great nations are founded or sustained.

But with dreams begin responsibility. We must look at the world as it is today and at the future as we can reasonably predict it will be. The open sea can be rough. Without venturing out, there is no journey and no accomplishment.

What we dream can make a difference—although sometimes we will never know how much. Every action we take, or fail to take, has consequences which run like ripples into the future. That future is limited only by our imaginations. Thus, we must form great expectations of ourselves and of Masonry, and then work to realize those expectations.

The past we honor proves we have been successful—the future we dream will determine our success in days to come.

We must not lose our heritage—the future of a tree is not assured by cutting off its roots. But we must not fail to see the future. Museums are filled with artifacts, which once met needs but failed to change the new expressions of those needs.

Dreams have power because they are reflections of our focus, and that power can be used for good. To intend well is important. To desire to make the world better for everyone is good and good comes from it. Regard the life of an Albert Schweitzer or a Mother Theresa, and the good becomes evident.

Dreams should be tested by looking both backward and forward: backward so that we can learn from our successes and be warned by the failures; forward so that our plans reflect the knowledge we have gained. If you decide to act on the dream, the difference between a future of strength and even glory and a future of decay and death by indifference can come down to one factor—your determination.

Rhetoric can inspire, but nothing impresses like hard, real actions. We should look for examples to men like ourselves who have gone beyond meeting everyday needs to fulfilling the dreams and aspirations we all harbor in our hearts.

Each of us can decide to fight one more day, each of us can postpone comfort, ease, peace, and security just a little longer—if we just stay focused on the dream. If we care more for the job to be done than our own recognition or comfort or ego (or fears), like Brother George Washington we can do great things.

Successful dreamers recognize the need to take stock, make plans, and then fulfill those plans. They don't wait for New Year's. Each day is an opportunity to reflect, resolve, and renew.

As individuals we can be fulfilled, happy, and prosperous if we nurture our dreams, then stretch our minds, hearts, and souls to embrace our personal infinite possibilities. United as citizens of this great nation, we can help fulfill America's potential for good—material, moral, and spiritual—in the world.

Our children are the dreams we send into the future, and the home is the foundation or all our tomorrows.

We sometimes forget that we are the ancestors of future

generations. Unless we create healthy families, a stronger Nation, and a better Masonry today, there will be no tomorrow for us. Let us never forget that our greatest glory as a freeborn people is to transmit that freedom to our children.

I am awed by my predecessors but none of us can rest on the laurels won by those who went before us. Our obligation is to continue their great work. The Grand Architect of the Universe has already given us eternal blueprints. Others have already built plumb and strong. We must follow yet improve, expand, adapt, and extract from the past the precious "gold" of inspiration and then mold it through practical application to our needs today.

In matters small and large, we all can, In Shakespeare's words, "Try the fair adventure of tomorrow." No excellence is possible without effort.

The story goes that Michelangelo was beginning a new sculpture from a monumental piece of marble. It was a particularly hard stone and flawed in several places. A fellow artist asked how he could hope to achieve his sublime vision with so difficult a material. "There is an angel within this rock," he answered. "All I have to do is set it free."

A grateful people are never satisfied with their yesterdays. The Scottish Rite sees man as alive with dignity, fraught with possibilities, and pregnant with the majesty of the future. Each of us can be a part of forever! In those, eternal dimensions lie the majesty of human dreams.

In the turbulent past, Freemasonry offered common ground where good men met on the square in peace and harmony. Today, as more and more people downshift from the frenetic pursuit of material gain to a larger sense of personal fulfillment, Freemasonry again stands ready to provide a shared vision whereby better, wiser, and happier men can build a better, wiser, and happier world.

Ideals

Those men with great ideals have been the ones who have made a lasting impression on the pages of the history of the human race. Every great advance in the cultural and political evolution of the race has come because there were those men who had noble ideals, lofty dreams, and courageous spirits; who dared chart their courses by some seemingly impossible dreams. People with great ideals have changed the boundaries of land, space, and time.

The future of our Nation and the world depends on the imperative of great ideals. It was men with great ideals who penned the immortal documents of our beginnings as a nation. It has been men with great ideals who, as soldiers and statesmen, have preserved for us the noble ideals of our beginnings.

The great ideals of life are things of the spirit and a new generation of Americans needs to rediscover the spirit that is to be found in great ideals.

# 22

Renewal

No business, no organization, no society, however powerful, will last indefinitely without developing a means for continuous self-renewal. All of our communities, whatever their scale or focus, are living things, and unless they find a reliable, reproducible way of staying young and vital, they are subject to the inexorable laws of aging and eventual death.

Change happens all the time, of course, and if it doesn't work for us, chances are good it will work against us. Unless we learn to manage change, we will eventually be swept away by it.

Management of change from without requires a creative response from within. But change for its own sake is as bad as no change at all.

The worst response we can make to change from without is fear. The most common ways to thwart change from within are to smother it beneath a pillow of tradition or bury it in a procedure.

Relevant organizations always survive and prosper; irrelevant ones become curious, quirky institutions, little more than sources for fond memories, museum exhibits and scholarly works.

Elders, as a rule, are fairly correct on matters of fact. What they may overlook is youth's vision on how facts can be built on and even altered to achieve unexpected and beneficial results. The ideal Brother is attuned to this delicate balance.

The result is more dynamic than mere compromise, fence-straddling, or fearful mediocrity. Rather, it is philosophy that conserves the best experience has taught while liberating us to seek the ideal.

It asserts that we have a reasonable control over our destiny. We are not slaves of fortune. We can change and improve both ourselves and our society.

There are some powerful precedents for the Freemasons as agents of change in modern society from before the nation's start. We were a major part of the creation of a new government on this continent—a government which put into its most basic legal documents the great principles of human freedom which fueled the Enlightenment.

We supported the documents in the Bill of Rights. Many of the ratification debates were held in Lodge rooms. Many Masons strove to bring about great change in the relationship of the government to the governed. And we won.

What Freemasonry did for the government of the greatest, most powerful nation on earth it can do for itself. And it can do the same for each and every member of the Scottish Rite who accepts renewal as a mandate and embraces it as an opportunity, not only for self-betterment but also for extended life.

23

Liberty

We teach opposition to any and all tyranny at any and all times—that any restriction on the speech or thought or belief of life of the individual is deeply suspect, and that the only legitimate restrictions on individual actions are those which prevent him from injuring another. That, too, is more important today than in the past, for as society becomes more complex, it becomes easier and easier for individual freedoms to be eroded in the name of social progress.

We teach that law is important, for it sets a standard of civilized organization. A Mason's sense of right and justice must go beyond the dictates of law (what is legal to do is not always right to do), but the law is always to be respected.

The joy of being helpful, the commitment to compassion and helping others, the opposition to tyranny, the importance of law—all are well-known life principles to the sincere Scottish Rite Mason. Our task is to find new expressions of these in the world and to strengthen them in our own lives.

If we believe in opposition to tyranny, let us be certain we do not wink at it in the world, and, even more importantly, let us be certain that we do not become petty tyrants to those around us.

The tyrant who masquerades as a leader cannot disguise the fact that his main purpose is to better himself and others to his will, for his benefit, not theirs. In contrast, the foremost thought in the mind of a Masonic leader is benefit to others.

The long history of humanity has been for the most part, one of fear of authority and the terror of the unknown. Humanity has come to see the unknown as a challenge and an opportunity, not a source of terror and dread. In this new equation, the great equalizer is human liberty.

The history of Freemasonry, by contrast, offers a portrait of the soul struggling against the flood tides of all those forces that would blight and destroy human personality. It is the eagle against the storm, the fish against the stream, and the soul against the world. It is the picture of man liberated from the bondage of little things and the tyranny of a dark future.

24

Industry

Mel Tillis

It is wrong-minded to suppose one form of work is more noble or elevated than another.

If you need a lifesaving operation, you are fortunate to have the services of a highly trained and knowledgeable surgeon. But you are also in debt to the workers who built the hospital, the custodians who keep it clean, the artisans who made the surgical instruments, and the research scientists in the pharmaceutical companies who created the antibiotics and other medications. And don't forget the nurses who monitor your vital signs and administer medicines, the workers who made the X-ray film, or the welders who put together the operating table. Without every one of them, you'd suffer potential consequences at least as serious as if the surgeon had never been trained.

Let your talents be known. Volunteer. Put your abilities

to work for your community, whether it's your church, your job, or a service organization like the Scottish Rite. Remember, when a person puts a limit on what he will do, he limits what he can do.

Your personal excellence can be the catalyst to make things happen. Your effort can be the added energy needed to succeed.

Is there only one way to really succeed in life—just one level of contribution that counts? Absolutely not! The road to success is always under construction and has many builders. Working as a team, we can all excel each in his own way.

Just as there are no unimportant tasks aboard a ship, so there are no unimportant tasks in Freemasonry. The fabric of the whole is strengthened or weakened by the condition of the parts. It really does depend on you.

25

Teamwork/Unity

Ours is a brotherhood without boundaries, faith without sect, and patriotism without party. Ours is unity of hearts universal, a bonding of good men becoming better though service to all humankind and the Creator.

For true success, we need "Dynamic Teamwork." Here group leader and team player are one and the same. Each Brother leads. Each Brother cooperates. The result is personal satisfaction and group accomplishment. Our dynamic brand of teamwork spells success, large-scale success, since the best abilities of every Brother are used to the fullest whether, for the moment, he is a leader or supporter, "chief" or "brave."

Freemasonry is friendship. It is an enduring bond built on shared knowledge, respect, and worthiness. It is the natural result of mutual striving in the good cause or our campaigns and becoming a community activist—these are the ways of a Mason. He does not destroy, but builds; he does not renounce, but reforms.

Masonry's unique mystique comes in large part, no doubt, from the simple wonder of our principles and shared fellowship. To the profane, it is difficult to understand how such a large group of men, vastly different from one another, can bond so closely.

The ties that bind Masons are the elemental, founding principles of our Order—and the acts that follow from them. In today's world where leaders often stumble and fall, family units dissolve and worthy causes suffer from a lack of interest or effort, Masonry keeps its light shining.

Unity

When, without thought, we all think alike, that is regimentation. When, against our will, we all submit, that is tyranny. When, of our free will and accord, we all agree that is harmony based on freedom and fulfilled by action. Clearly, the latter is Masonry's ideal of unity.

Unity is the cornerstone of the Masonic movement. We cannot—we must not—sacrifice this firm foundation on which so many have built, and built grandly, for so many centuries. Unity is a landmark that guides. It is a touchstone that separates the genuine from the false.

Freemasonry espouses the ascendancy of man's spirit and rejects purely materialistic theories of human nature. Our Craft teaches of a silver cord, a transcendent bond of brotherhood, binding all men. From distant ages to modern times, our Craft has recognized the basic unity of all men, both in theory and in practice. Thus, our Order brings men together, irrespective of race or religion, into one common bond, the mystic tie of Freemasonry.

The strong thread of unity is most obvious in Freemasonry itself. Here it can work most freely and effectively since every person involved is a Brother and has taken his oath at a Masonic altar to revere the Creator and serve his fellow man. Thus, there is a harmony within the Craft. Brothers agree on all essentials. It is only a matter of applying these principles to the case in hand whether it is, for example, how to assist the local public school system, observe a patriotic holiday, promote a worthy charity, or contribute to a Masonic program.

Just as the Venus de Milo, however excellent it is in part, would be perfect and complete if it were whole, so each body within Freemasonry is only complete when it is united with the entire Fraternity. If we accent one segment of the Craft to the exclusion of the rest, we splinter and weaken the totality of Freemasonry. Our work is too great, too important, too needed. We cannot become divided. Our harmony, our Masonic unity, is imperative.

Our work is great. But we must work together to achieve the success we envision. United for the common good of all, we can share common goals and together accomplish uncommon heights for our Craft and our Nation.

Together we rededicate ourselves to unity in fraternal relations, unity in positive public profile, unity in service to our communities, and unity in harvesting the mutual benefits of our Masonic bond.

When we are tempted to focus on what divides us as opposed to what unites us, Masonry offers a great admonition, "Build bridges, not battlements."

Inside Masonry, we agree the first political task is for each Mason to gain control of himself. After that, our second labor is to benefit our Brothers and others in every way we can. Toward this end, as willing individuals, we cooperate for the common good.

In Masonry, the only requirement is to believe in God. The details of faith are for the individual to resolve in his soul and his house of worship, not in the Lodge room of the Fraternity. Good men can belong to different faiths, for almost all faiths contain great and important moral truths.

Masonry calls men to look for what we have in common, not for what divides us.

Torn between good and evil, apathy and action, man must fall back on the still voice of Deity speaking to his inner self and gracing his existence. This internal, always-present guide is never wrong if correctly heard. Freemasonry turns our ears, as well as our minds, to this quiet inspiration. This is why Freemasonry is so important. Its lessons point the way beyond division to unity. It links, even bonds, the dynamic, yet often opposite, poles of life.

Masonry provides a philosophy and a fraternity where good men can "meet on the Level and part upon the Square." It binds all men in a mystic tie of sincere brotherhood and mutual love. Faith and work, soul and body, as well as heart and hand are united as Masons everywhere labor through Freemasonry in peace and harmony to honor the Creator and serve mankind.

26

Fellowship/Listening

Sincere fellowship: Nothing is so valuable and so rare in the hustle and bustle of today's busy world. Conversely, jealousies, petty rivalries, little islands of self-interest, and the like simply damage everyone.

To impugn someone's character or undercut a budding project are petty triumphs that jealous people daily feed on. The jealous person is, in the end, mocked by his own fault. He is never happy, never content. Rather than truly accomplishing something, the jealous person is negative and counterproductive. He finds fault. He points out errors. He makes fun of enthusiasm. Always negative, envy does not build. It destroys.

Tragically, it not only defeats the best intentions of others but also works on the jealous person himself, killing with venom any shred of self-respect he once might have had. Envy, like fire, reaches upward and attempts to bring down those who have excelled.

There is nothing constructive about jealousy. It continually tears everyone and everything down to the dead level of the envious person. Because envy's malignant energy is spent destructively, the jealous person receives no benefit at all. He is left empty and discontent. He soon gains a reputation as a "sour ball."

Despite its great power, jealousy never accomplished anything of value. Envy and discontent go hand-in-hand with self-service, diminishing both their owner's humanity and the dignity of others. In the final analysis, jealousy is really guilt—at not being as good as others, or as energetic or dedicated.

By contrast, happy, confident, and sharing people working in true fellowship contribute to the betterment of all.

Listening

The straightest path to real growth is to listen.

In every conversation, the listener has much more to gain than the speaker. The speaker is just stating what he already knows or thinks he knows. The listener is learning. He is absorbing new facts and ideas. He is judging and sorting them. He is getting much more out of the situation by listening than by looking for an opening and taking the opportunity to vent his own views.

We should listen even when we're speaking. One of the best indicators we have for enthusiasm is our own voice. Learn to listen to it, to really hear it. What does it say? You will be amazed when you hear the message under the words.

Compliments are fine. They give a boost to your spirit and point out directions to follow. Also, they're easy to remember. But complaints are just as important, perhaps more so. They underline perceived errors and call us to reconsider our policies. Brushing complaints aside is no solution. You have to listen to every point of view.

If we can accept the opinions of others and give proper credit to their ideas, our own minds are opened to fresh perspectives and possibilities. We break the prison of our own egoistic, narrow viewpoints and are better able to understand the perspective of others.

27

Optimism/Reason

A n optimist is someone who sees the good, even the best, in a situation. A Mason, by definition, is an optimist. He does not live in the past or react to the present with knee-jerk reflexes. He uses the past creatively to seek a better future. He takes advantage of opportunity, making it work for himself and for the Order.

The optimist has a rational grasp of present possibility. He acts and is not discouraged if the result is less than he had hoped. He knows that something is gained by action, while nothing can be gained by apathy and inaction.

Optimism is the philosophy of builders. One brick in place, one line complete—that is enough to justify the optimist. He cannot and does not expect to build a magnificent temple by himself. But he can shape the stone at hand truly and place it square.

Pessimism fulfills its own prophesy and is self-defeating. The pessimist is fixed on the mud and declares no area fit for construction. Preferring the hole to the doughnut, he disregards the optimist as, simply, someone without much experience. In truth, experience is a hard teacher, and its lessons can appropriately chasten the fanciful dreamer of impossible schemes.

The success of every good cause depends on the work and time of dedicated volunteers. Through these workers the cause is benefited, but the individual gains even more. Personal worth is firmly reestablished and there is a fresh sense of self-respect. New possibilities for growth emerge.

To dismiss something as "impossible" is to admit defeat without a fight. It's a word we can do without, for diligence and skill, energy and dedication can achieve the impossible.

Optimism is a characteristic of youth. Pessimism is associated with old age. In fact, real age is basically irrelevant. One can be young at 80 or ancient at 20. It is all a matter of attitude, of mind over matter.

Sustaining an optimistic outlook is the key to success. It calls for a balance of metaphorical age and youth, of hopefulness and deliberation. Perhaps, the best approach to that balance is to be one who strives, not only to change the entire world, but also to make present conditions better.

We should not expect overnight miracles. Nor should we sit on our hands and complain about the impossibility of accomplishing anything. Rather, we should realistically gauge the situation, exert our best effort, and then build on the progress of those results.

This is an age of pessimism. Every newspaper headline screams danger. Every newscast is draped in the sable gowns of melancholy. History is caught in the gloom of a terrible whirlpool of repetition and destruction. Art today as represented by modern painting and sculpture is, so many times, a wild disarray of clashing colors and ghastly caricatures of human life. Music is no way out. And the psychologists, so often, crown the whole with their doctrines of futility. All of human life seems to be engulfed in Arnold Toynbee's "Rhythm of Disintegration."

An optimist is someone who sees the good, even the best, in a situation. And isn't that the central philosophy of the Scottish Rite? We take good men and make them the best men possible.

Reason

Every world or major philosophy ultimately simplifies to a few fundamental maxims that are basically the same. "The Golden Rule," in one phrasing or another, has been advanced by great writers and thinkers of every age, from Pythagoras and Cicero to Spinoza and Goethe. Human consciousness and conscience in age after age have come home to values that all good men can accept as touchstones of truth.

The common element in these universal and eternal values is reason. They make sense, bring results, and create happiness.

We must never cease our opposition to superstition, no matter how wrapped in profit or pseudo sanctity it may come. While superstition as a game may be a source of quiet humor, superstition as a force in the lives of men and women, especially superstition confused with faith, is always destructive. Superstition is incompatible with reason.

In stressing reason and moderation, Freemasonry acts as an effective counterweight to extremism of every sort.

Guided by reason, not driving by passion, our lives become more productive, our relationships more harmonious, our minds more open to what, together, we can achieve for ourselves, and our fellow human beings.

28

Honesty

The old admonition is right that the love of money is the root of all evil, but money itself is innocent. By the same token, those who make money should be admired for their industry, and not taken to task for the violation of a misunderstood and often misquoted adage. The wise person uses every legitimate and honest means to earn a living. The real issue of right or wrong revolves entirely around how the money is made and used.

Just as money can be a true and faithful servant, it can also be a harsh master. The rich man is a pathetic fool if he serves only himself and places making money in any way possible above making it honestly.

In his famous *Essay on Man*, Alexander Pope said, "An honest man's the noblest work of God." The reverse is also true. The dishonest man is the vilest work of evil. Honest men rightly scorn him. His efforts at social climbing and conspicuous consumption are valid targets of ridicule.

Private property forms the basis of individual wealth, but it is our obligation to use that wealth wisely and justly. The answer to economic injustice is not communism but compassion, not government confiscation but individual caring, not income redistribution but devotion to charity.

Selfish or self-serving actions have a price, and that price can be very high. The man who spends his life thinking about and acquiring great wealth may suddenly realize he has acquired it—and lost friends, family and joy in the process.

29

Gratitude

Gratitude is many things. There is a purpose at the heart of all life. History is the grand and glorious revelation over the centuries of a plan for the heart and mind of man to grapple with and to work for the fulfillment of a dream of a world in harmony with the Divine plan. Every successful encounter with life and every achievement of a noble dream is a cause for thanks.

We live in an Age of tremendous happenings for which we are truly thankful; but there is more! There are yet horizons of the future for the exploration of the vastness of space and the probing of the causes of human conflicts. A grateful people accept the challenge of their tomorrows, not with fear, but with courage and confidence.

Appropriate gratitude to our Creator and to our forefathers involves a commitment on our part as a free people to work for the good of all mankind. We cannot afford to bask in our blessings while others suffer. At the heart of all our philanthropic efforts is a humble sense of thanksgiving.

30

Caring

Senator Bob Dole

When was the last time you stopped to ponder the real meaning of our country's great national holidays? For too many Americans, Independence Day is a little more than a time for fireworks and cookouts, and President's Day is an excuse to go shopping for a car. The world has grown indifferent about the human bravery that made us free and careless about the values that have made us great. The sound of volley and trumpet from our once honored past have faded from the public consciousness. America's great milestones have been noisily preempted by a blurred succession of commercialized and secular holidays.

At the same time, our preoccupation with pleasure and profit has blinded us to the injustices and creeping tentacles of competing ideologies which threaten to make a mockery of sacrifices of our heroes of the past. Forget the memories of our legacy and we become easy prey for those who would destroy us today.

Indifference and apathy go hand-in-hand. Like smoke, apathy obscures the issues. When nothing is clearly seen, nothing is done.

Even more destructive than the lethargy of apathy is active negativism, the self-defeating attitude of simply complaining without any move to correct errors and make things better.

Mason's know the importance of a dynamic, constructive posture toward people we serve, the values we embrace, the tasks we set, and the natural heritage with which we have been blessed. Once these twin dragons of apathy and negativism are eliminated, a beneficial positivism can take their place and result in real gains.

In particular, Masons care about the environment. Just as Masonry fosters the unity and cooperation of all humankind, so too does our Craft encourage us to unite in revitalizing our precious natural legacy.

Freemasons have never embraced patriotism, service, or environmentalism as fads that are allowed to fade into the background when something else comes along. Instead, the community of man and nature has been and always will be an integral part of who we are as Masons and what we seek to accomplish on this, our Mother Earth.

Moderation

A sure way to undermine Masonic good cheer and help-fulness is to give undue weight to angry or abrasive persons. These types of people offer little to others. Their petty vendettas and self-interested harpings are useless. The fruit of their arduous labors is hallow and without savor, for if they make some small gain, it still raps on their egos since they think they deserve so much more.

Avoid them. Leave them to their own self-bred poisons, for the only thing sure about this type is that they will fail and bring you down with them if they can. Seek the company of positive, cheerful people who see the good in others because it is so abundant in themselves. Be sure your own mood and mien reflect these same Masonic values.

Beware of their opposites: the love of power, status, and physical possessions. Left to themselves, these worldly desires will drive and dominate our lives.

Our nobler passions do not drive us. Rather, they guide us. Patriotism, altruism, and compassion, for instance, offer us polestars that point to our higher potentials. They lead us away from excess, selfishness, and an adversarial relationship with the world, and toward the deeper satisfactions that come through love and loyalty.

The one element essential to controlling human vices and exalting human virtues is moderation. It is the key to a well-balanced, harmonious, and productive life.

Friendship

The people you associate with make all the difference in the world. They have a great psychological influence on you, and you on them. You affect each other's conscious minds, and more subtly, your respective subconscious minds. Friendships are precious, but some contain unseen pitfalls.

The most potent form of leadership has always been by example. That means that everything you say and do in the view of others is subject to interpretation as a model of Masonic values and actions. You want those words and deeds to reflect the highest possible standard.

It is the best hope of good people that they will have a positive effect on the lives of those around them. But the same dynamic is always potentially at work in both directions, and none of us can afford to be around people who aren't cheerful, positive, enthusiastic, and motivated by a generous spirit. If you can't change them, leave them alone. They cost you too much—in money, in achievement, and in peace of mind.

Don't forget, the other people in your life are leading by example as well, even if both of you may be unaware of their power and their purpose.

33

PEACE

The unrealized dream of the human race is for a world at peace. The dream lives on in the hearts of all who cherish the dream that the entire world will learn to live together as one, in love and unity. In particular, peace on earth is a dream deeply embedded in the hearts of all Masons.

The forces and resources of Freemasonry have been and always will be dedicated to the noble purpose of making peace in our time a reality. It will be a peace that is born of liberty in the hopes of men everywhere.

It will be a peace of truth, wisdom, integrity, tolerance ... and all the other virtues listed in this small book. It will be a peace born in the example of our Creator and nurtured in good hearts throughout the world.

APPENDIX

The articles in this book represent my husband's thoughts over many years. He shared these thoughts with his Masonic Brothers. Even though some subjects are repeated, each article represents a real insight into the subject being presented.

* * *

The New Age, July 1986

America the Beautiful, the Bountiful

It is a paradox of human nature that we must lose something before we value it. For example, the ill truly appreciate good health; the beggar really knows the value of money; the blind realize the preciousness of sight. This paradox also applies to love of country. We treasure America most when we are abroad. In fact, I doubt that anyone who has not left our shores can fully realize what America means. Perspective clarifies vision. Absence brings realization.

Note what happens when Americans meet in a foreign land. There is an instant affinity. We have found in another person a fragment of America. The bond is immediate and strong. We share at once a common heritage and feeling. We are Americans—and proud of it! Distant from our home, we know its virtues more keenly than ever. For this reason, everyone should travel. If not abroad, then at least out of our familiar surroundings.

The key is to see freshly. Consider your daily routine. In your walk or drive to work, do you really see people, buildings, and parks you pass? Probably not. They are just part of the background. Your true vision is, most likely, fixed on the day's obligations, what tasks you have to complete, what people you have to see. You miss the real beauty and significance of your immediate surroundings.

Break the routine. Take a new route. Even your hometown will seem suddenly seem different—and better. Then take a trip through your State or see an entirely different section of America. Visit the South, the North, the Great Plains States, the Pacific Coast. See a part of America you never visited before. You will realize more than ever just how beautiful and bountiful America is. Going abroad is even more startling. The majority of the world's people live without what we as Americans take for granted. You see the obvious, of course. In fact, often there is poverty and deprivation. Nowhere in the world is the common man better off than in America.

Where we have adequate food and shelter, they have poor nutrition, even famine, and inadequate housing. America's great natural diversity and beauty is paralleled by bounty previously unknown to the world. Only 15% of the average American's income is used to purchase food. This is possible because America has the most productive agriculture in the world. Compared to any other nation, Americans produce larger better and less expensive yields per acre. American technology—whether in agriculture, industry, or electronics—also lands and vast resources allowed phenomenal growth. Today, we continue to compete and improve in an international market where only excellence can survive.

But America is more than natural beauty and material bounty. Freedom is our most precious heritage. Where Americans have freedom of expression and lives lived in liberty, many peoples across the globe bear the heavy weight of tyranny and endure lives governed by fear and repression. In America, we have free media able to report without censorship and the liberty to speak our mind. We have greater individual rights than ever experienced in the history of mankind. So long as we do not interfere with the rights of others, we are free to pursue our dreams. Capitalism, for instance, is economic democracy at its finest. And if there was a transgression of rights, the American way is "innocent until proven guilty."

The cornerstone of these personal freedoms is the Constitution. It has stood the test of time and remained the fundamental law of our land for nearly three centuries. There have been changes, of course. But the Amendments to the Constitution have, in fact, expanded American liberty and prosperity. They have never changed the essential structure of this immortal document. As Freemasons, we can be especially proud, for the Constitution in large part was formed by Brethren according to the principles of our Craft. Brother George Washington was the presiding officer of the Constitutional Convention, and Brother Benjamin Franklin was the elder statesman. Washington's leadership and Franklin's guidance stamped Masonry's hallmark on the Constitution. Since then generations of Brethren have labored to keep America free and strong.

As Americans and Freemasons we share a double glory and duty. Sons of this soil, we are indebted to America for its bounty and opportunity. Brothers of Freemasonry, we are America's staunchest supporters since our Nation comes closest in the history of mankind to fulfilling our Craft's ideal vision of the Brotherhood of Man under the Fatherhood of God. And the end is not in sight. As the poet said, America is "Time's noblest offspring." We are now reaching for the stars, and despite setbacks and sacrifices, we will succeed. I am proud to be an American. Equally, I am proud to be a Freemason. Most of all, I am proud to be a Freemason living in America. This double heritage is mine-is ours-to nurture today and to extend to tomorrow.

C. Fred Kleinknecht

* * *

The New Age, July 1987

Let's Tackle the Task!

One of the rich rewards of being Grand Commander of our Jurisdiction of the Scottish Rite is to be able to visit with my Brethren in the various Orients throughout the Southern Jurisdiction. It is a special joy to be able to visit with my Brethren here in the Orient of Panama. I am grateful for the opportunity to come and be with you and to assure you of my appreciation for all that you are doing for the Scottish Rite and of my continuing interest in the work of this Orient. You have been and continue to be a vital part of the work of our Jurisdiction and I want you to know that we in The Supreme Council are proud of you labors.

It was the dream of some men who said: "Let's dig a ditch across this span of some 44 miles" that has had a tremendous impact on the history of this century in the life of the Americas, and in a sense, in the life the world. It was that great American Freemason, Theodore Roosevelt, who had a great part in making the dream of a waterway connecting the Atlantic and the Pacific oceans a reality. We may never know to what great extent Freemasons contributed to the building of the Canal, but we can be sure that they were among the dreamers and the toilers who made a dream come true.

I am sure that some laughed at those early dreamers who said: "Let's dig a ditch" through the jungles of a narrow slip of land that would serve in peace and war to bring the people of the Americas closer together. It was for some, I am sure, an "impossible dream," but strong men and great minds dared to believe in the impossible, and so we have today the wonder of the Panama Canal. Some of us in the States are sorry that politically the Panama Canal is separated from the Nation that gave the Canal birth, but we are proud of the fact that, Masonically, you are still a part of us!

I feel that it is imperative that we always have the spirit which says of the seemingly impossible; "Let's dig a ditch" and get on with the task of making a dream come true. There will be obstacles and difficulties in the pathway of the fulfillment of our dreams, but I trust that we will be the men of this time in history who will possess the courage and the will to overcome and get on with the business of building a better world and a better tomorrow for all mankind.

I have to come to visit with you, to renew some old acquaintances, and to make some new friends as I get the chance to shake your hands and chat with you. However, I have come for something more. I want to share with you something of concerns and programs of your Rite. We wish you to know what we are doing and what we are trying to do to further advance the work of the Scottish Rite in our Jurisdiction. We have dreams and each of you can have a part in the fulfillment of those dreams.

Your Supreme Council is concerned about promoting growth in membership, not only in the Rite, but also in all bodies of Freemasonry. WE are not content to sit by and accept the disturbing losses in membership in the bodies of Freemasonry and do nothing about it. We are making available much material that can be used in enlightening non-Masons on the subject of Freemasonry and hopefully thereby encourage them to seek to become one with us. If Freemasonry and the Rite are to show an increase in membership, it will be because we are motivated to do something about declining membership. We must redouble our efforts to enlarge the ranks of Scottish Rite Freemasonry from that great reservoir of Freemasons who have not yet joined our ranks. I would hope that this Orient and all the Orients in our Jurisdiction would make the gaining of new members one of their first priorities in this New Year.

Your Supreme Council continues its endeavors to promote the principles of liberty and freedom for all peoples of the world. In the States, we are working with the Bicentennial Commission on the 200th Anniversary of the signing of the Constitution of the United States, the celebration will be in the year 1987, 200 years after the signing in 1787. That Constitution was and is "the Keystone of Liberty," and the principles which if promulgated are those principles which can assure any free people stable and free society. Through education and *The New Age*, we will be doing much this year to bring to the attention of all our Brethren the vital importance of making liberty and freedom a major concern of freedom loving people everywhere. I encourage and challenge all Scottish Rite Masons everywhere to be ever vigilant in the defense of liberty, for liberty is a hallmark of Freemasonry and the Scottish Rite. We dare not take our liberty for granted and this calls for renewed dedication to the teachings and principles of the Scottish Rite where tyranny is despised and liberty is championed!

Your Supreme Council is involved in a great program to help others! Our children's hospitals, our program for treatment of children with learning disabilities, our scholarship programs, and the philanthropic work in the many Orients serve to project an image of the Rite which says that our hands of help and encouragement are extended; wherever, there is a need to be met. We are proud that our efforts are making it possible for little children to have a better life. We are proud of the part we are playing in furthering the education of some of our finest young people in order that they can make a worthwhile contribution to the tomorrows in the life of our world. I am glad to report that your contributions to the various programs of the Scottish Rite are paying dividends in the smiles on the faces of little children and in the achievements of young men and women who are now making their mark for good in our world today. We must be ever willing to "go the second mile" in helping others, for then we will be taking another giant step toward making the "brotherhood of man under the fatherhood of God" a reality.

There is so much more that I could say about the work of The Supreme Council, but I wish to close my remarks on a personal note!

I am proud to be your Grand Commander, but I am most proud of the fact that I am one with you in the bonds of fraternalism as a Mason. The doors of your Grand Commander open from the outside, and I am ready at all times to lend a listening ear to your suggestions and, if need be, to your criticisms. I want you to feel that my office in the House of the Temple in Washington is a place where you will always receive a warm and cordial welcome if you visit Washington. I am grateful for all your kindnesses to me and assure you of my brotherly love for all of you who are a part of this Orient and our Grand Jurisdiction.

We look back to the past with pride. We face the future sure that our tomorrows are bright with promise. I ask only that you join with me in all our efforts to further the advancement of the human race on this globe, and I trust that our beloved Scottish Rite will always be in the forefront of every noble cause.

Thank you. And now, we walk together into our tomorrows.

C. Fred Kleinknecht

* * *

The New Age, July 1988

Only Through Masonic Unity Do the Best Get Better

Samuel Clemens was fond of telling stories about the American West where he, as a young reporter in Nevada, began writing under the name of Mark Twain. One of his most famous anecdotes is about the richest man in a rough-and-tumble Western boomtown. Because this sturdy pioneer wanted to add some "class" to himself and the growing town, he decided to decorate the rooms of his newly built home with copies of some classic statues from Italy.

In time, the pieces arrived after each endured a rough stagecoach ride across the American plains. Upon uncrating the largest piece, one labeled Venus de Milo by the Italian shipper, the rich man discovered a statue without arms. Mistakenly convinced it had been a damaged in shipment, he took the local postmaster to task—and collected damages! Content with his compensation, the man began to look at the statue more kindly, and soon he liked it just fine, believing that the arms, if it had any, would just be useless additions.

Today, are some of our Brethren like this purblind gentleman? Have these Brethren become so involved in one aspect of Masonry that they have forgotten how important each part is to the whole of Freemasonry? Just as the Venus de Milo, however excellent it is in part, would be perfect and complete if it were whole, so each Body within Freemasonry is only complete when it is united with the entire Fraternity. If we accent one segment of the Craft to the exclusion of the rest, we splinter and weaken the totality of Freemasonry. Our work is too great, too important, too needed. We cannot become divided. Our harmony, our Masonic unity, is imperative. If one group breaks off from the rest, every group is affected and so, ultimately, is the Symbolic Lodge, the foundation of all Freemasonry.

We must never forget that the Symbolic Lodge is the core of our Craft. It is the foundation upon which all else in Freemasonry depends. The basic, universal, and eternal lessons of the three degrees form the sound foundation upon which we build our lives. In our lodge, we become Masons in our hearts. No other degree is more important, for the principles of the Lodge bring us integrity and strong character, dignity, and respect. In return, we strive to be of service to others through our charitable endeavors and our steadfast concern for individual liberty and freedom.

For those Brethren who wish to extend themselves further in Masonry, there are the Scottish Rite and York Rite. Here, the lessons of the Lodge are expanded through ritual. Here, the scope of Masonic Fellowship is widened to include more Brethren who wish to become even better through living and sharing their dedication to Freemasonry. Yet always a Brother is reminded that he is first a Mason of his Symbolic Lodge and only then a member of the York Rite or Scottish Rite. These additional degrees only expand one's horizons and opportunities. They do not change the compass direction set in the Entered Apprentice, Fellow-Craft, and Master Mason Degrees, without which there can be no true progress in the Craft.

Many Thirty-second Degree Scottish Rite Masons as well as many Knight Templars choose to become Shriners. By making the condition of Scottish Rite or York Rite membership, a prerequisite for becoming a Shriner, the Shrine becomes a unique and even stronger organization. Its members already have acquired a deeper understanding of their symbolic Lodge teachings through participation in the Scottish Rite and/or York Rite. They are the seasoned timbers with which yet greater Masonic accomplishments can be achieved. The inner temple of commitment can now manifest itself in endeavors of even wider significance, such as support for the Shrine's outstanding Hospitals for Crippled Children and Burns Institutes.

Nor does the impact of Freemasonry stop here. There is the opportunity for participation in many other Appendant Masonic Bodies, each truly outstanding in its own province. Consider the Tall Cedars of Lebanon, the Grotto, the National Sojourners, the High Twelve, and the many other noteworthy Masonic related groups. They all contribute magnificently to the betterment of others and our Nation. Masonry works in hundreds of ways to meet special needs and helps those who would otherwise remain unassisted.

Consider also the great founding document of our Country, the Constitution. The American statesman Salmon P. Chase described it saying: "The Constitution in all its provisions looks to an indestructible union composed of indestructible States." Similarly, Freemasonry is an indestructible union of indestructible Lodges and Appendant Bodies. United, we work together in a diversity of ways to achieve one goal. Divided, we weaken the whole of Freemasonry and lessen the effectiveness of each separate part.

Those who desire to exercise their own authority in a limited scope adhere to the maxim of "divide and command." A better motto, and one at the heart of Freemasonry and every true Brother, is "unite and guide." Let us, then follow the ideals established in the Symbolic Lodge. Let us build on them, in all the diverse ways that contribute to the benefit of Freemasonry. Our work is great. United for the common good of all, we can share common goals and together accomplish uncommon heights for our Craft and our Nation. As Henry Wadsworth Longfellow wrote:

"All your strength is in your union,"

"All your danger is in discord."

C. Fred Kleinknecht

> *This article was written prior to the change in Shrine rules dropping Scottish Rite and York Rite membership as a prerequisite for Shrine membership.*

* * *

The New Age July 1989

July 4th—The Birthday of an Immortal Document of Freedom

The great documents of history have shaped the destiny of men and nations. The writings of prophets and poets, sages and philosophers, statesmen and scholars, as well as soldiers and saints have motivated men in their search for truth, freedom, and faith. Someone once wrote: "The pen is mightier than the sword." A study of history will reveal that victories of history have been won by the mind, spirit, and pen of men who have put down on parchment the best dreams and aspirations of mankind.

We read of a touching incident relating to the actual signing of the Declaration of Independence. On the morning of the day it was adopted, the venerable bell ringer ascended to the steeple, and a little boy was placed at the door of the hall to give him notice when the vote was concluded. The old man waited long at his post, saying, "They will never do it, they will never do it." Suddenly, a loud shout came up from below and there stood the blue-eyed boy, clapping his hands, and shouting, "Ring! Ring!" Grasping the iron tongue of the bell, backward and forward the old man hurled it, 100 times, proclaiming "liberty to the land and to the inhabitants thereof."

A small unknown blue-eyed boy and an unknown bell ringer heralded the beginning of the end of the rule of a tyrant. The hurricane of war, with all its perils and sufferings, was yet to come, but down the road there was a victory for a just cause and the birth of a new Nation where all could enjoy the blessings of "life, liberty, and the pursuit of happiness." The Liberty Bell has been silent for many decades now, but we trust that Americans will always be the bell ringers for freedom and liberty for all the peoples of the Earth.

The Declaration of Independence remains a viable and crucial document because of the spirit and commitment of its singers, who mutually pledged to each other their lives, their fortunes, and their sacred honor. Their lives were endangered, their fortunes lost, but to their everlasting glory, it can be said that they never lost their sacred honor. They were sought by the enemy as traitors, yet they never betrayed their commitment to the principles of freedom and liberty. They were among the great patriots of the Revolution.

Thomas Nelson, Jr., one of the signers and later Governor of Virginia, lost his home in the closing moments of the war. During the siege at Yorktown, he observed that though the Americans poured shot and shells thick and fast into every part of the town, they seemed carefully to avoid firing in the direction of his house. Governor Nelson inquired why and was informed that his house was being spared out of personal regard for him. He immediately ordered them to disregard the fact that it was his residence, and at once, the military began to pour shells into his home. Clearly, the penned words of Jefferson were signed by men who had courage and conviction to defend to the death, if need be, the principles of that immortal document.

July 4, 1989, will be a day of celebration as the Nation pauses to recall the momentous events of its beginnings, its immortal documents of freedom, and the drama of a revolution! There will be fanfare, fireworks, and festivities. There will be parades and parties. There will be speeches and spectacular events. There will be a holiday, and sad to say, it will be, for some in our Country, no more than a holiday.

We in the Ancient and Accepted Scottish Rite would call on all Freemasons and our fellow countrymen to make this Fourth of July a day of remembrance and a time of reflection when we once again visit in our memories that hallowed place in the history of our beginnings as a Nation of free people. I trust that this July 4 will remind us that great minds and great hearts have given us much to be thankful for! The dreams of the signers of the Declaration of

Independence were fulfilled in the victory at Yorktown and in the writing of that "keystone of liberty," the Constitution, which said that "a new nation under God" had been born.

There is, in another sense, a dream yet to be realized. We enjoy the blessings of "life, liberty, and the pursuit of happiness," but we must realize that the dreams of the Founding Fathers will never be fully realized until it is true that "life, liberty, and the pursuit of happiness" are not just the past but continue to be always in the forefront of all those who work and pray for the ultimate fulfillment of the American dream of freedom and liberty for all men everywhere.

C. Fred Kleinknecht

* * *

The Scottish Rite Journal—July 1990

Dominoes of Tyranny

The cherry blossoms came early to our nation's capital this year. Suddenly bursting into brilliant whites and pinks, the trees around the Washington Monument and the Jefferson Memorial at the Tidal Basin were glorious. Capital residents caught unaware by the instant beauty seemed to see them for the first time. Tourists reveled in the unexpected bonus.

Freed of the beauty queens, brass bands, and costumed parades scheduled for weeks later, the lovely trees displayed pure, unembellished beauty. Their message of peace and international cooperation, as originally intended when the trees were given to America by Japan, came through clearly without the interference of television cameras, crowds, and politicians.

What was looked at was, for once truly seen. After a quiet walk under the bright fleecy boughs, people left deeply inspired, more aware than ever before of the strength, resilience, and beauty of nature. They saw with fresh eyes man's place in the scheme of things—to cultivate and nurture the good and true, the basic and eternal in life.

Is there lesson here that goes beyond blossoms? I think so.

Too often we clutter our lives to the extent that we see only the surface and not the spirit within. Take our holidays, for instance. The true meaning of Christmas is often lost in concern for giving the appropriate gift or having a snowfall on that special day. At Easter, the message of spiritual regeneration is confused with superficial symbols of physical renewal—eggs, chicks, bunnies, and lilies.

The Fourth of July is no different. Amid the bunting, flags, fireworks, and iced watermelons, our sense of what our nation's birthday is all about seems to get lost. Picnic arrangements and parade-side seats distract us from the real meaning of the Fourth.

This year other nations have forcibly reminded us of what the Fourth of July is all about. In Eastern Europe, country after country has freed itself from decades of Soviet domination. Once we feared the "domino effect" and were convinced that if one country fell to world communism, others would follow in quick succession.

Today, however, the dominoes are reversed. The Soviet client state of Cuba stands alone in the Caribbean. Nicaragua moves swiftly toward democracy. Poland, Hungary,

Romania, Czechoslovakia, Lithuania, and other Eastern Block nations that fell under the Russian yoke after World War II have broken with Moscow and even rejected the ruling elite of their native Communist parties. The dominoes of tyranny are toppling.

For four decades, America longed for and worked for this rebirth of freedom. But few really expected it—certainly not so instantly and broadly. Like those bursting cherry blossoms in Washington, suddenly liberty is blooming, free political systems are taking form, people born under repression are finish the line from the next page.grasping with relish an idea as old as mankind but one our forefathers, so many of them Masons, brought with fresh vitality to our world on that famous July Fourth over two centuries ago: "We hold these truths to be self-evident, that all men are created equal, that they are endowed by their Creator with certain unalienable Rights, that among these are Life, Liberty and the pursuit of Happiness."

Here is the essence of every July 4: Life, Liberty, and Happiness. These are the true values of our Independence Day. Just as religion needs no priest or church, patriotism needs no politician or parade. This holiday, lets' celebrate the real Fourth. Let's realize—as people all over the world are now coming to understand—that freedom is a principle beyond price. That it will forever blossom in the human heart. That we, as Americans and Freemasons, are the modern guardians of an ideal to which all mankind has always and will always aspire.

Fireworks dazzle, but then fade. The flame of freedom is strong. It may flicker, but it is never extinguished. Celebrate that flame this Fourth of July, my Brethren. But also guard it and live it. Through our acts, let its beams reach throughout the world and bring the light of Life, Liberty, and Happiness to all mankind.

C. Fred Kleinknecht

* * *

The Scottish Rite Journal—July 1991

Environmentalism: Brotherhood in Action

A cid Rain, Smog, Water Pollution, the greenhouse effect, and extinct and endangered animals—in recent times, the focus of America and indeed of the world has been on the declining state of our planet. Billions of dollars and endless hours of research are spent each year in analyzing the effects of pollution on the environment. Huge rallies have been organized, such as Earth Day here in Washington, D.C., to raise public awareness and support. The involvement is great, often drawing big name stars and hundreds of thousands of "earth activists."

There are, however, other members of the population who do not seek high publicity and extensive media exposure. Instead, they work every day trying to make a difference, however small by solving local problems and uncovering answers to our environmental dilemma. They work quietly and often without recognition. I am pleased to note that many of these people are Brothers. Masons across America and in every corner of the globe are becoming more aware of the problems facing our natural community and are stepping forward to help.

Recently, a conference was held in Seattle, Washington,

called "Brotherhood in Action: Interdependence in an Emerging Global Society." This international meeting of Brethren was designed to review two subjects basic to Freemasonry: humanity's place in and responsibility for the universe.

One speaker, Dr. George A. Seielstad, a professor of Astronomy and a National Science Foundation Fellow, posed this problem. "One species, *Homo sapien,* has acquired sufficient power to act with global consequences. Yet this power has accumulated so rapidly that humans have not acquired experience to manage it; neither do we have the luxury of waiting until our wisdom matches our capabilities."

The chairman of this conference, Stephen Schafer, 32°, emphasized the importance of environmental action now: "The content of this conference is basic and intrinsic to Brotherhood and Freemasonry. It will give us a new perspective, based on recent scientific discoveries, on our universal principles of Brotherhood, and ... our responsibilities in an emerging global society."

President Bush concurs. In section six, "Now or Never," in the television series "Race To Save our Planet," he said: "I do care and it is essential we all care." Clearly, the hour of decision for our survival is at hand.

The theme of Masonic involvement in our natural community is evident in our own publication, *The Scottish Rite Journal,* where recent issues have underlined examples of Masonic ecological awareness. In the June 1990 issue of *The Journal,* Dr. Melvyn N. Freed, 32°, K.C.C.H., expressed grave concern about pollution in his article "An Act of Reclamation." He asked "What can we, as Free and Accepted Masons, do to salvage our inheritance, Mother

Earth? I urge that we separately and collectively accept leadership in developing programs of reclaiming our environment, our natural heritage."

Similarly, in this issue, the article "A Tree Grows in Isreal," by Rabbi Sidney S. Guthman, D.D., 32°, K.C.C.H. (page 20), discusses the importance of reforestation. In addition, "Demolays Hike Yosemite" by Bro. Kenneth N. Cooper, 32° (page 64), as well as "Meeting in the Sky" by John R. Horton, 32° (page 1), accent Freemasonry's role in developing among Masons an appreciation of our natural environment.

What can we all, as Masons, do to save our earth, the greatest of natural resources? Perhaps, we could start a local renewal project, such as Brothers of Harmony Lodge No. 340, Pikeville, North Carolina, who initiated an "Adopt a Highway" program. As noted in the "Of Current Interest" section of the May 1990 issue, these concerned Brethren maintain the cleanliness and beauty of their local road systems.

In fact, they further improve and protect the natural area around the highways by clearing away refuse, much of it potentially hazardous, and then encouraging the regrowth of native plant life. In addition, much of the material they collect can be recycled, and the resulting funds donated to a local cause, often a Scottish Rite Childhood Language Disorders Center. Thus, two worthy goals are achieved—America's handicapped children are aided and our environment is improved! Since the publication of the above article, I have received letters from many other lodges throughout the Southern Jurisdiction, each with its own "Adopt A Highway" or other environmental program.

Robert Burns, renowned eighteenth century poet and

Masonic Brother, wrote of his concern for the environment in this verse: "I'm truly sorry man's dominion has broken nature's social union." Similarly, the twentieth century horticulturist, Ill. Luther Burbank, 33°, troubled by the devastating effects of pollution on the plants he experimented with, created hybrid strains of vegetation which produce their bounty faster and with much greater resistance to air and water pollution. These Masons, living centuries apart, were conscious of a problem which today has taken on disastrous proportions. Just as Masonry fosters the unity and cooperation of all humankind, so too does our Craft encourage us to unite in revitalizing our precious natural environment.

For Freemasons, environmentalism has never been a craze which eventually fades into the background when another project comes along. Instead, the community of man and nature has been and always will be an integral part of who we are as Masons and what we see to accomplish on this, our Mother Earth.

C. Fred Kleinknecht

* * *

The Scottish Rite Journal—July 1992

The Little Lodge That Could

As Grand Commander, I am privileged to receive bulletins and other news materials from many Symbolic Lodges, even small ones, from across the Southern Jurisdiction. Recently, a phrase in one of these caught my attention. It was BLU LOJ, phonic spelling for Blue Lodge.

It is on the auto license plate of Jim Presgraves, Secretary of Mt. Airy Lodge No. 226, Rural Retreat, Virginia. He's had the plate for years.

Hooked by those two words, I read the entire *Trestleboard* of Mt. Airy Lodge and then requested a history of the Lodge from its Worshipful Master. It soon became clear to me that Bro. Jim's license plate underlines the dynamic Masonic spirit of this small rural Lodge in southwestern Virginia. Because of the many outstanding activities of its members, I call this fine group of Masons "The Little Lodge That Could." What can they do? Here are a few examples— all from one Lodge meeting!

They can raise new members every year, more than enough to offset losses.

They can have an officers' line where the average age is in the mid-30's.

They can do Degree work for other Lodges, whereas a few years ago they depended on other Lodges to help them per-form Degree work.

They can, on a typical Lodge night, vote financial support of Job's Daughters, the Children's Miracle Network Telethon, and the Masonic Home of Virginia.

They can, on that same night, look back at a successful spa-ghetti supper which netted funds to support their Lodge and its philanthropies while, at the same time, serving "the best spaghetti they've ever eaten" to their neighbors and guests at the Rural Retreat Community Center.

They can thank their youthful Worshipful Master, Wor. David Miles Harlow, 32° and his wife, Gail, for making the sauce, Bro. George Washington Pennington for washing the dishes, and Rt. Wor. Charles Martin "Charlie" Cassell, 32°, for mopping up.

They can volunteer to prepare food for and manage barbecue, coleslaw, and soft drink booths at the upcoming Rural Retreat Fair, July 14–18.

They can arrange for a fundraising auction at a busy local crossroads of items donated by the Brethren and accept the offer of Bro. Gregory Todd Hash, 32° who is a volunteer fireman, to use the Rural Retreat firehouse for the auction in case of rain.

They can sign up to six volunteers to assist Bro. Rodney Eugene Hurt, a 20-year Lodge member who is also Rural Retreat's Maintenance Supervisor, and his municipal crew in repairing the sidewalk outside the lodge.

They can thank Wor. Paul Lee Humphreys, 32°, and his wife, Maxine, for donating the framed Masonic art prints "The Lodge Room Over Simpkins Store" to the Lodge.

They can announce the regular fellowship meetings of members are in nearby "Granny's Kitchen" (where peanut pie is a specialty) at 6:00 PM before Stated Communications.

They can thank Rt. Wor. Jack Vipperman for organizing a well-attended bus trip to Grand Lodge.

They can welcome Wor. Charles Gordon "Harry" Hoback, Jr., 32° Instructor of Work for the 42nd Masonic district in Virginia and Honorary Member of Mt. Airy Lodge, for attending their Lodge often and working with the Brethren to develop word-perfect Ritual.

They can arrange, at the urging or Rt. Wor. James Richard Rowe, 32°, District Blood Program Coordinator, to meet the regional quota of 100 pints.

They can listen to the positive reports of six members regarding the second reading of a young petitioner and vote his acceptance.

They can pass a get-well card for everyone's signature and arrange how to get a handicapped Brother to Lodge.

They can respond with interest to well-prepared reports by Wor. Willy Andrew Wilson, 32°, district Education Officer, and Bro. James Owen, Lodge Masonic Home Ambassador.

They can (after all the above!) have a period of warm fellowship and hearty refreshments after Lodge.

Clearly, they can be proud of their 86 members representing nearly every walk of life: farmer, salesman, landscaper, building contractor, police officer, funeral director, Methodist minister, retired U.S. navy aviation officer, antiquarian book seller, and Clerk of the Wythe County School Board.

Mr. Airy Lodge No. 226 is truly a little Lodge that can. Why? Because its leaders and members, many of them also Scottish Rite Brethren are dynamic, enthusiastic, dedicated Masons.

It has not always been so. The Lodge, founded in 1875, often had to struggle to survive. To make ends meet, its lower floor, once a free school and a church, has been rented out from time to time as a warehouse, a motion picture theater, a U.S. Post Office, and now a small engine repair shop.

Yet, the Lodge can count among its distinguished members Ill. Bro. Thomas Bahnson Stanely, 33°, former Governor of Virginia, 1954–1958, and Bro. C.D. Doak who served as

Secretary of State of the United States.

Today, typical of the commitment of its Brethren, Mt. Airy Lodge has two members serving as Grand Lodge Officers in the Grand Lodge of Virginia, has Brothers waiting in line to be Lodge Officers, can perform all three Degrees without outside help, has an informative monthly *Trestleboard*, and consistently has fine speakers, interesting programs, and meaningful community involvement such as participation in the Virginia Grand Lodge's Child Identification Program.

No wonder I call Mt. Airy Lodge No. 226 "The Little Lodge that Could"! Your lodge can, too! After all, success comes in cans, not cant's!

C. Fred Kleinknecht

* * *

The Scottish Rite Journal—July 1993

Pretty Good Is Not Good Enough

There once was a pretty good student, who sat in a pretty good class, and was taught by a pretty good teacher, who always let pretty good pass.

The above is the opening passage of a poem Bro. Robert David Pogue II, 32°, now Past Master of Teikoku Lodge No. 19, Grand Lodge of Japan, quoted during his message at the January 1992 installation banquet of the Scottish Rite Valley of Kitanakagusuku, Orient of Okinawa.

This pretty good student lived in a pretty good town and

graduated from a pretty good school only to find, when he started looking for a job, that "pretty good might not be good enough." Indeed, getting a job was tough.

The moral is in the poem's last stanza: "There once was a pretty good nation, pretty proud of the greatness it had, which learned much too late, if you want to be great, pretty good is, in fact, pretty bad." My thanks to Worshipful Brother Pogue for his reminder.

At last, confronted by quality automobiles form abroad, America is now aware that "pretty good" in not good enough, and the United States is now producing cars where "quality is job one." Similarly, there is, among other positive trends, a new dedication to providing quality healthcare to every American and bringing our national influence to the forefront in regard to the recently independent countries of Eastern Europe. Significantly, Scottish Rite, S.J., has been central to this new birth of freedom, especially as seen in the recent restoration of the Grand Lodges in Hungary, Poland, Czechoslovakia, and most recently, Romania.

Similarly, Scottish Rite support by both Northern and Southern Jurisdictions undergirds the vision of Freemasonry in the year 2000 as developed by 30 Grand Jurisdictions of North America, the Imperial Shrine, and the Grand Encampment in part three of the Masonic Renewal Committee's strategy as announced after the October 27–29, 1991, meeting in Tulsa, Oklahoma.

Clearly, quick-fix solutions do not work in either worldwide or American Freemasonry. Now is the time to stress quality in:

- Membership enhancement strategies

- Masonic leadership skills

- Community and family involvement

- Development of a global, united Fraternity.

How we can attain these goals was recently outlined in part, by Ill. Kees J.P. van Boven, 33°, Sov. Gr. Comdr. of the Netherlands, at the 38th Conference of European Sovereign Grand commanders. Also, the Masonic Renewal Task Force is presenting package programs containing videotapes, print support materials, and comprehensive guidebooks. Each is focused on a specific issue. Together, they present a practical vision of Freemasonry's role in service to the individual and his society. The programs accent Masonry as an organization of high ideals with practical reasons for belonging; an organization that respects an individual's time and commitments; an organization that provides family and community focus; an organization that offers informative, rewarding, and entertaining experiences; an organization that delivers on its promise of providing opportunities for fellowship and shared accomplishment with men of good moral character and high principle.

In other words, quality control must be an essential part of our Craft today.

For centuries, Freemasonry has declared itself the largest and most humanitarian Fraternity in the world. Today, however, as demits multiply and membership either languishes or just holds on, we have to realize that declarations are not deeds, that if Freemasonry is to succeed in the twentieth century, we must innovate quality controls NOW. There is no time to lose. We cannot leave one good man outside our ranks because we did not give him valid reasons to petition.

We must realize that a "pretty good" Fraternity will produce only "pretty good" results. We have been the best, we should remain the best. Let us make others realize that fact by reviewing who and what we are, by taking the steps to improve the quality we need in members, programs, and goals. Let "quality is job one" be our standard in every area of Freemasonry.

Pretty good is not good enough for Freemasonry or for you!

C. Fred Kleinknecht

* * *

The Scottish Rite Journal—July 1994

Join A Winner!

By providing a focus on the history of our Order and on related Masonic subjects, the Scottish Rite Research Society fills a significant gap in Masonic study—and does it with style, spirit, and scholarly excellence.

Frankly, I didn't expect such enthusiasm. Suddenly, however, Brethren were coming at me from every direction!

The place was Irvine, California. The day was April 16, 1994. The occasion was the Scottish Rite Workshop for the Northwest and Southwest sectors. After a telephone conference with Ill. Warren D. Lichty, 33°, S.G.I.G. in Nebraska and President of the Scottish Rite Research Society, all the details were in place.

With pride and a sense of importance of the moment, I announced to the assembled Brethren incentives which will accomplish two things: (1) increase membership in the

Scottish Rite Research Society and (2) sustain the Society's present scholarly excellence.

The quality of the Society and its publications is well established. Approved at the 1991 Biennial Session of The Supreme Council, 33°, the Society has already produced one volume of transactions. Titled *Heredom*, this premiere volume, contained a wide variety of outstanding essays ranging from Professor C. Lance Brockman's well-illustrated study of Thomas G. Moses, a scenic artist expert in J. Robinson's incisive essay "Albert Pike and the Morning Star." Back issues of volume one of *Heredom* can be purchased only by members of the Society. Copies are still available for members.

The second volume of *Heredom* is nearly complete. It contains, among other excellent offerings, a beautifully illustrated essay on Masonic Furniture, a thorough study of the Royal Arch Word, insights into Pike's Thirteenth Degree Lecture as used by the Supreme Council for Iran in-exile, and a view of contemporary American anti-Masonry from the perspective of Europeans who experienced the Nazi attack on Freemasons during World War II.

In addition to its transactions in softbound and available deluxe hardbound editions, the society published a newsletter titled *The Plumbline* which, like *Heredom*, is edited by one of our Rite's and Freemasonry's most outstanding scholars and writers, Ill S. Brent Morris, 33°. Nor is that all. The Society has also distributed to its members complimentary books such as *Masonic Philanthropies* by Dr. Morris and *The Bible in Albert Pikes "Morals and Dogma"* by Dr. Rex R. Hutchens, 33°, and the reverend Donald W. Monson, 32°, K.C.C.H.

By providing a focus on the history and Ritual of our

Order and on other related Masonic subjects, the Scottish Rite Research Society meets a continuing need in Masonic study—and does it with style, spirit, and scholarly excellence. The Research Society is already a success. As Honorary President, first Charter Member, and first Life Member of the Society, I heartily congratulate the Society's present 420 members. More than that, I am fully behind a new incentive program to expand the membership and benefits of the Society. Remember membership or subscriptions are available to all interested parties—Scottish Rite Masons of any jurisdiction, Master Masons, and non-Masons alike.

Our goal is at least 3,000 members, and to accomplish this, the Society's President and Board of Directors have approved the following provisions effective from April 16 to December 31, 1994:

- Waiving the usual $35.00 joining fee.

- Reducing the annual membership fee to $20.00 for 1994.

- Distributing, the 1994 bonus book with each new member.

- Establishing a Life Membership for $300.00

Within minutes after the announcement of these membership incentives at the Irvine, CA, Scottish Rite Workshop, 38 Brethren joined the Society. Also, three Brethren became Life Members. In addition, I personally sponsored 12 new memberships. Within 10 minutes, the Society grew over 10%.

Becoming a Scottish Rite Research Society member during this special incentive program is more than a bargain. It is a significant contribution to the scholarship of the Rite and to your understanding of our great Scottish Rite traditions.

Join a winner! Become a member of the Scottish Rite Research Society today. And sponsor others! It is a bargain. It is a benefit to you and the Order. It is the best thing any Brother can do to extend the Scottish Rite tradition of intellectual accomplishment into the twenty-first century!

C. Fred Kleinknecht

* * *

The Scottish Rite Journal—July 1995

It All Starts With the Father

Patriotism, love, and loyal support of one's country.

It's deep within our minds, deep within our history, and deep within even our language—this association of our fathers with our nation. The Latin word "father" is not only of "patriotism" but also of "patriot" and "patriotic." Nor is it only the Latin-derived English words which follow the pattern. We also speak of the "fatherland."

Clearly, in nearly every culture on record, love of one's country is an outgrowth and reflection of love of and respect for one's father.

None of this should suggest women are, in any way, less patriotic, less filled with "love and loyal support of one's country." The great women patriots, from ancient Sparta to those who served in Desert Storm, are shining examples of the devotion of women to their native land.

But sociologists tell us most children learn their attitudes toward their country from their fathers. For Freemasons and members of the Scottish Rite of Freemasonry, there are some important implications in this fact.

The Scottish Rite has always stressed the importance of patriotism. Albert Pike, for instance, wrote in *Morals and Dogma*: "Above all, the Love of Country, State Pride, and Love of Home, are forces of immense power. Encourage them all. Insist on them in your public men." Also, again and again in the Degrees of the Rite, the candidate is reminded he must love his nation and constantly see how to improve it.

But how? How can we serve our nation, especially in those happy times when there are no major wars to be fought, nor enemies to be defeated? In wartime, patriotism is self-evident. One fights! Or one supports those who have gone to fight. In peacetime, patriotism becomes a more subtle virtue, and the question is how to demonstrate it on a practical, day-to-day basis.

It all starts with the father

If it is true young people learn their attitudes toward their country from their fathers, then our most vital task is to be the fathers who teach those attitudes. Even if our own children are long since grown, we can still find ample opportunity to teach by example of our lives and by the respect we show for law and for individual freedoms. These ideals, especially toleration, are the essence of our great nation. If we cherish and live these values, so will our young people. Similarly, they will value the nation which protects and represents these values.

There are many such opportunities. We can work with the Masonic youth groups as friends, Dads, and advisors. We can give volunteer time to Scout troops, serve on community projects that benefit youth, and teach the young in our houses of worship. We can serve as block parents or assist in the schools.

Doing so, we become living examples of Masonry, of care and compassion, and of dedication to the rights of the individual. We can teach more patriotism in 10 minutes of living values America represents than we can in 10 weeks of shouting at the young that they had a better love America or leave it.

Most men may not think of it as an act of patriotism when they help the young to read, or resolve conflicts, or find the strength to do what they know is right-but it is, perhaps, the purist act of patriotism a man can perform. Whether with our own children or with the youth of the community, we can serve as role models of the attitudes America cherishes. We can inspire the young with our lives, as thousands of generations of fathers have done before us.

It all starts with the father.

It all starts with you.

C. Fred Kleinknecht

* * *

The Scottish Rite Journal—July 1996

You Sometimes Wonder

You sometimes wonder why it matters so much. It's only a piece of cloth, printed in red and blue, with white showing through the stars and stripes.

It doesn't matter because of its intrinsic value—a few dollars at most. It doesn't matter because of its design. You could not call it ornate—its more nearly like an abstract design. It doesn't matter if it's functional, for it isn't. The fabric isn't thick enough to keep you warm. It isn't waterproof enough to shelter you from the rain.

And yet it matters; it matters a great deal. It doesn't have the intrinsic value of a Jaguar, or a diamond, or even a Mickey Mouse wristwatch. And yet no car or diamond, or time-piece ever inspired the warmth of affection, that sudden catch of breath which most Americans feel at the sight of the flag of the United States flying free in the wind.

It is not ornate or decorative as most of the architecture over which it flies, yet catch a glimpse of it, silhouetted against the sky at sunset, or in the glow of the first rays of dawn, and rare will be the man or women untouched by its beauty. And although it is not functional, even the most practical and hardheaded of us treasure it more than the efficient machinery on which we so much depend. Somehow, we feel we would give up the machinery, if we had to, but not the flag. So why does it matter so much?

It matters not because of what it is, but because of what it means.

Of little intrinsic value itself, yet the flag symbolizes the protection of all intrinsic values. The economic and personal freedom it symbolizes assures us that our property is secure. No one, least of all the government, can arbitrarily take your property from you, and the full power of the government will fall upon anyone who does.

Not itself highly ornate, the flag not only guards the treasures of art and architecture of the past, but also guarantees that the creative spirit of mankind shall run free to create beauty and greatness for the future.

And it symbolizes the ultimate in functionality as well. It is as functional as the most modern factory, as practical as birth, as useful as farmland, because its shadow protects these things and so much more.

So the flag does matter. Not what it is, but what it means— not for how it looks, but for how we see it—not for what it does, but for what we do in it name and under its protection.

Let us be proud of that flag and of what it symbolizes. It matters because we matter, because every man and women and child in the country is precious, and what they produce by the sweat of their brow or the inspiration of their mind is precious. That, in the simplest terms, is the answer.

It matters because we matter.

It is precious because we are precious.

It is the symbol our people. It matters because of you.

C. Fred Kleinknecht

* * *

The Scottish Rite Journal—July 1997

"America the Beautiful"

Almost everyone knows the verse of "*America the Beautiful*," the immortal song by Katharine Lee Bates. It begins with the words:

O beautiful for spacious skies, for amber waves of

grain, For purple mountains majesties above the fruited plain!

Fewer of us, however, are familiar with the third verse:

O beautiful for heroes proved in liberating strife, Who more than self their country loved, and mercy more than life! America! America! May God thy gold refine, Till all success be nobleness, and every gain divine.

It could be argued that this verse is the most Masonic stanza of the song—that it sums up the Masonic attitude toward patriotism. For when Masonry speaks of patriotism, it is not speaking of a mindless and unthinking devotion to country, or some sort of reflex reaction at the sight of our flag. These unworthy of thinking men and women.

Patriotism, for a Mason, involves conscious and deliberate choices, not automatic conditioned responses. Bates writes that America is beautiful for heroes who were tested and proved in a battle not for land, or power, or conquest, but in a battle for liberty, for an ideal, a vision of human dignity and potential.

These heroes, and heroines, loved their country—that is to say the ideals of freedom, the right of the individual to self-determination in political, religious, social, and intellectual matters—more than they loved themselves, and loved "mercy more than life." That is to say, they valued compassion, caring, and charity more than mere existence.

Those sentiments of true patriotism could have come from any of the Degrees of the Scottish Rite. We are taught that "Liberty, Equality, and Fraternity are the foundations of a free government," that "Man assumes his proper rank as a moral agent when with a sense of the limitations for his nature—arise the consciousness of freedom, and of the obligations accompanying it," and that "charity, clemency, and generosity are essential qualities of a Mason." Bates then writes:

> America! America! May God thy gold refine,
> Till all success be nobleness, and every gain divine.

She is alluding, of course, to Malachi, the last book of the Hebrew Bible: "He shall sit as a refiner and purifier of silver: and He shall purify the sons of Levi, and purge them as gold and silver, that they may offer unto the Lord an offering of righteousness." (3:3) She hopes that God will so purify the thoughts and actions of America that its every act will be an acceptable offering; that any success an American might hope for would be a noble success, a success which was not personal nor selfish but intended for the benefit of others.

And again, the Scottish Rite teaches that our thoughts should be for others, not ourselves. Perhaps, the most famous quotation of Albert Pike, engraved in the wall of the House of the Temple above his bust, is "What we have done for ourselves dies with us. What we have done for others and the world lives on and is immortal." This is the "gain divine," the "offering in righteousness."

This, then, is patriotism as Masonry understands it. It is a conscious, thoughtful dedication to the welfare of others, the people who comprise the nation. It is the heroism of men and women who are prepared to offer the sacrifice of their own lives that others may enjoy the benefits of liberty. Patriotism, a cardinal virtue of the Mason, is the honor we pay to the past and the hope we express for the future.

C. Fred Kleinknecht

The Scottish Rite Journal—July 1998

Great Expectations

We should expect more, not less, from Freemasonry.

"Get a Life: Thoughts on Freemasonry and Religion" is a new pamphlet published by the Masonic Information Center. It is reprinted in this issue. I'm proud to say the Southern Jurisdiction of the Scottish Rite had a strong hand in its preparation. Its major themes of aspiration and toleration are certainly central to the philosophy of our Order. But I was especially struck by this passage from the pamphlet:

What are some expectations Freemasons have of their Fraternity?

Masons have many expectations of their individual faiths, but these are entirely personal matters outside the scope of a fraternity. What a man expects of the Masonic Fraternity is clear.

- An opportunity to form friendships with men of different backgrounds in education, occupation, and religion.

- A way of learning about himself, of taking a personal inventory of his strengths and weaknesses among friends.

- Opportunities to make a difference in the community.

- Friends to whom he can "let off steam" or discuss his problems.

- An opportunity to learn leadership skills and develop self-confidence in dealing with people.

- A journey of self-development which includes all aspects of his nature.

- An affirmation of values derived from the human experiences of many cultures over many centuries.

- A sense of being connected with other men who share his values.

- Help and support in times of personal crisis.

- Basically, help in getting a life of excellence and fulfillment in this world.

Granted, these are powerful words that express powerful ideas.

I wonder if some of us err by expecting too little from Masonry. Certainly, Masonic writers and thinkers have told us over and over again that we find what we seek in the Fraternity. Perhaps, we do not always seek enough.

I know from my own experience and from the experiences of Masonic friends that the list of expectations above is realistic. I have the privilege of knowing men from many different backgrounds—good men it is a pleasure to know and whom I would never have met without the Scottish Rite. I have experienced the humbling but very healthy experience of seeing great men and great ideas portrayed in our Degrees. As with all thoughtful men, Masonry has given me many opportunities to make a difference for good. The genius of our Fraternity is that it gives that opportunity to *every* Mason who is willing to take it.

The other expectations are real, too. And they are truly met by the person who seeks them. The Fraternity does all this well, but it can do it better! As we plan for the twenty-first century, there are two basic questions we must ask and answer:

- How can we encourage men to ask more of Masonry?

- How can we do a better job of meeting the needs and expectations of our membership?

The 1998 Scottish Rite Leadership Conferences have addressed those questions. The Strategic Planning Subcommittee of The Supreme Council, chaired by Ill. C.B. Hall, 33° S.G.I.G. in West Virginia, has also these issues in its excellent report during the 1997 Biennial Session. Similarly, thoughtful men in the Grand Lodges, Scottish Rite Valleys, Masonic Districts, and local Lodges across America are wrestling with the same crucial matters.

Just asking the questions is nearly a Masonic miracle. For generations, the questions would have been unthinkable. Now we have come to understand the great truth that "the future will happen; the only question is whether it will happen *with* us or happen *to* us."

That future will be determined by our expectations. Expectations are among the most powerful shaping forces in the world. Imagine what would have happened if Mozart's father and teachers had expected him to be only an indifferent musician, or if Illustrious Brother Harry S. Truman's parents had expected him to be just an average athlete. We all know of instances in which the expectations of a single teacher have raised the performance of an entire class.

Our future is limited only by our imaginations. Thus, we must form great expectations of ourselves and of Masonry, and then work to realize those expectations.

C. Fred Kleinknecht

* * *

The Scottish Rite Journal—1999

At The Turning of the Stair

Each year, the Supreme Council sends a beautiful calendar to every member of the Scottish Rite, Southern Jurisdiction, and to many friends of our Order. The 1999 calendar's cover features the massive bust of President and Brother George Washington in the gardens of the House of the Temple, and the photograph for the month of July shows the turning of the Grand staircase as it ascends from the Atrium to the Temple Room in the House of the Temple in Washington, D.C.

The turning of the stair is a fitting image for July, the month we most associate with patriotism. For the Declaration of Independence on July 4, 1776, the founding of the United States was in every sense, a turning of the stairs.

Until then, the history of the world had followed a more or less straight line—a set of variations on a theme. But then, in Europe, the Enlightenment movement of the Eighteenth Century grew from a tiny spark to a glowing coal, to a roaring flame, casting new light on man's social, religious, intellectual, and political status. And Masonry was the forefront of that movement. Margaret Jacob has traced the importance of Masonry to the spread of the Enlightenment in Europe in her book *Living the Enlightenment*. Steven Bullock, in *Revolutionary Brotherhood*, has shown the importance of Masonry in the founding of the United States. Both books should be a "must read" for all Masons.

The Enlightenment brought new ideas into the world. They seem commonplace and obvious to us now—we are, after all, children of the Enlightenment—but they were truly revolutionary at the time. Paraphrased, among these ideas were the following: Man has both the right and the ability to control his own destiny. No one has the right to tell anyone else what to think or believe. The right to govern comes not from divine right but from the consent of those being governed. Each person has the right to meet with others any time and any place he wishes. Each person has a right to an opinion and to express that opinion, even if it is contrary to the wishes of government, the teachings of the church, or the values of others. The state is the servant of the people— the people are not the servant of the state. Anyone can own and read any books he wishes. Every person has a right to security in his or her home.

We hardly need to think about those great ideas. They are so much a part of daily lives and experiences that we simply accept them as "the way things are." Recent events, however, tell us that things are not that way, at least not everywhere. If you would realize just how fortunate we are, consider the plight of the Kosovar refugees. It is impossible to understand—almost impossible even to consider.

It seems that the stair is turning again, and turning toward an inhuman cruelty, we thought had passed forever into history. But there are some turnings of the stair that history cannot be allowed to take.

And should you ever doubt that the teachings of the Scottish Rite are important to the world today—pressingly, desperately relevant—consider Kosovo. If you doubt that there is still need in the world for dedicated and informed men to champion toleration and political freedom and the rights of men and women to be secure in their own homes, again consider Kosovo. Freedom is never free. But the loss of freedom costs more than anyone can afford.

The world stands, again, at the turning of the stair. And now, as always, we will need patriots to guard the stair and keep nations free.

C. Fred Kleinknecht

* * *

The Scottish Rite Journal—July 2000

Masonic Unity The Right Choice

Over the past few weeks, many Masons have been considering the question of Masonic Unity. The Internet has literally hummed as masons from many different Masonic organizations have debated the question. Often, the exchange has generated more heat than light.

And yet light is badly needed. The history of Masonry has shown over and over again that there truly is strength in Unity. Thus, in this publication and in the *Northern Light*, Masonic leaders have stressed the importance of Unity—of never forgetting that the Blue Lodge is the foundation of the entire Masonic family and that support of the Blue Lodge is critical.

In fact, just a few months ago, the Southern Jurisdiction released a new videotape, *Architects of Freedom, The Story of Freemasonry in America*. Produced with care and at considerable expense, it focuses on Masonry, the entire family of the Craft, not just the Scottish Rite. It is designed for loaning to friends, to tell them about Masonry, or for use in Friends Night at Local Lodges. The price of the tape was deliberately kept low ($10 a copy) so that individual Masons could easily afford to buy and give away copies. The tape, which has won three film awards, has been very well received by the Brethren.

Both Jurisdictions of the Scottish Rite, as well as the Shrine and other Masonic Bodies, have helped to fund the Masonic Renewal Committee of North America in the development of membership enhancement and retention materials. Where they have been used, these materials have proved successful. In these and other ways, the Scottish Rite has been advancing Masonry-all of Masonry. But true Masonic Unity involves more than the commitment of leaders and financial resources. True Masonic Unity requires the commitment of the individual Mason. For, in the final analysis, you and only you can make a difference. We can produce programs, videotapes, and information packets—but unless you talk to your friends about Masonry, unless you tell them why it is good and that you would like to share Masonry with them—then all we can do amounts to little. Grand Lodges can offer Lodge leadership training programs which can make a great difference for any Lodge. But unless you attend those programs and put what you learn there into practice in the leadership of your Lodge, the effort and expense are futile.

Masonic Unity begins in the heart of the individual Mason. It comes from a deep knowledge that Masonry is *good* and *does good*. It comes from a personal commitment to Masonry prospering as a whole and to making that happen. It comes from a determination to become personally involved in that Unity, that growth. It means that you will talk up, not down, every Masonic Body, whether you are active in it or not. We are a family. We must support each other fully, unconditionally.

YOU literally make the difference in Masonic Unity. There are things which could and should be considered at the national level—a public awareness campaign, coordination of efforts, and increased philanthropic outreach. But Masonry grows when you talk to a friend about the Fraternity, give him a petition, and bring him into the Blue Lodge. You can do that, but without you, nothing will happen.

Those are the alternatives. We can work together, and we can bring our friends into the Fraternity. If we do, Masonry—all of Masonry—will not only live, it will be better than ever before. In contrast, we can do nothing or, worse yet, we can undermine by talk or action the Masonic Unity which has been the tradition and strength of our Craft from its beginnings.

It shouldn't be a hard choice to make.

C. Fred Kleinknecht

* * *

The Scottish Rite Journal—July 2001

What So Proudly We've Hailed

My duties occasionally take me to the Archives of the House of the Temple, and recently, I was there to look through some of the past issues of the *New Age Magazine*, as the *Scottish Rite Journal* was titled until January 1990. Many Brethren may not realize how long the Southern Jurisdiction has been publishing "a literary monthly magazine" as a means of "communication between the brethren of the Rite throughout our vast jurisdiction" and for "the education of the people in the highest sense." Whether titled the *New Age Magazine* or the *Scottish Rite Journal,* we have published a jurisdiction—wide magazine since June 1904. Indicative of its central purpose as a means of general education, the first issue, 144 pages long, included a variety of materials—art sketches, science, social service, poetry, and short stories—along with an article about the House of the Temple and 30 pages on specifically Masonic subjects.

From then to the present, many Grand Commanders have written messages, such as this one, and many more Scottish Rite Masons have shared their beliefs, ideas, and research with the Craft through the articles they contributed to our magazine. Running through all those years and those millions of words, like a bright thread in a tapestry, is the theme of patriotism, a theme still of central importance to Scottish Rite Freemasons everywhere this Fourth of July.

For nearly a century in this publication, we have proudly hailed our country and our flag. It is not surprising that the Scottish Rite has made such a point of patriotism. Albert Pike himself wove it into the rituals and the teachings of the Order. On page 156 of Morals and Dogma, he writes: *The true Mason identifies the honor of his country with his own. Nothing more conduces to the beauty and glory of one's country than the preservation against all enemies of its civil and religious liberty. The world will never willingly let die the names of those patriots who in her different ages, have received upon their own breasts the blows aimed by insolent enemies at the bosom of their country.*

Grand Commander Pike honors those willing to defend our country at all costs. But he also stresses it is just as important to remember that the glory of a nation is not only in its battles but also in its administration of justice and the care it takes of all its citizens. Mercy, humanity, and compassion are essentials of true patriotism.

In this sense, patriotism has been the theme uniting the hundreds of articles published by the Southern Jurisdiction over these many decades. We proudly hail those men and women who have fought our country's battles. At the same time, we honor as patriots those who have championed justice, humanity, freedom, religious toleration, and equality. The poet Frederick Gillman captured the sense of the Scottish Rite patriotism when he wrote: "*God send us men with hearts ablaze/All truth to love, all wrong to hate:/These are the patriots nations need;/These are the bulwarks of the state.*"

The Scottish Rite will continue to accent the responsibilities of citizenship and the practice of the great personal and civic virtues which alone can make a man, or a nation, great. We will continue to provide educational materials to our youth, telling them the great story of our nation and our flag. We will proudly hail in the future, as we have in the past, those who have made a difference for good in the world. For this, as Pike understood, is true patriotism. Through nearly two centuries of existence and 97 years of publication, the Scottish Rite, S.J. United States, has carried the central message of patriotism— great men and women make a great nation. May each of us continue to strive for that greatness this Fourth of July and always.

C. Fred Kleinknecht

The Scottish Rite Journal—July 2002

America Is As Strong as Ever!

The Terrorists of 9-11 failed to understand that America is not only a mighty power but also a country of great people who unite in the midst of disaster.

Ten months have passed. Sometimes, the events of 9-11 seem to have happened long ago. At other times, it is as if we can still see the twin towers of the World Trade Center crashing to the ground in gigantic clouds of fire and dust; the Pentagon in flames; the plane crashing in Pennsylvania. Like most Americans, I am trying to come to terms with all the changes that morning made in my life, but I know life will never again be the same.

For a person, as for a nation, there are times that redefine everything. For a man, it happens when he marries, when his first child is born, and when his father dies. The loss of his father forces him to realize, often for the first time, his own mortality. In these times, something of innocence is lost and something of a deeper, more permanent character is gained. Priorities shift. Values are redefined.

So, it is for us as Americans. On September 11, we suddenly became aware of our national mortality. We could be attacked, even inside our borders. We could be moved from being seekers of success to a people fearful of unknown terrorists. All priorities changed on September 11. The great majority of those changes have been positive. As a nation, we had been powerfully focused on the quantity of life. Now, we have learned to focus more on the quality of life.

Since 9-11, we have seen an outpouring of charity and an almost unprecedented willingness to get involved. The people of our nation dug deeply into their pockets to help the families of those whose loved ones were lost or injured in the terrorist attacks. Men, women, and children pitched in and helped, naturally and automatically, from the very heart of their humanity. In a spirit of true patriotism, people have responded with an outpouring of emotional capital, empathy, and compassion. There have been parades, speeches, and commemorative events. Men, women, and children now proudly display the flag more than any time since the end of WWII. It is an inspiring sight, and my heart beats with pride more than ever when I see "Old Glory" given its due respect.

We have rightly made heroes of those who ran again and again into the burning buildings in the hope of saving one more life. We honor those passengers on Flight 93 who heroically saved the country from further disaster. We cheer our young men and women of the military as they go to foreign lands to teach the marketers of terror that they cannot and will not succeed. We have committed ourselves to war against terrorism wherever it may strike.

The terrorists made a fundamental mistake. They knew we were a mighty power. They failed to understand that America is not only a mighty power but also a country of great people who unite in the midst of disaster with a greatness of mind, heart, and soul. Beyond the flags, slogans, speeches, and anthems, there is the dedication of a free people to the truths which make them free. These truths are the source of our greatness. America is as strong as every!

C. Fred Kleinknecht

The Scottish Rite Journal—July 2003

America the Land of Choice

The glory of America is that we have made the choice to be great and accepted the responsibility of that choice.

If you were to ask me what makes America great, I would answer, "it chooses greatness." In the early days of our nation, Americans had the rare opportunity to choose, and that opportunity, continued today, has transformed our history as a nation.

There were few choices for the British subjects of the 1600s and the 1700s. If your family owned land and you were the firstborn son, you inherited the land and were expected to stay there and manage it. If you were the second son, you probably went into the military as an officer. If you were the third son, you almost certainly went into the church. A maverick son might break the pattern and set sail for Australia or the American Colonies to make his fortune. But, by and large, opportunity was determined by the chance of your order of birth, not the personal choices you made. If your family were not of the landed gentry, your fate was even more dictated by chance. If your father farmed, you farmed. Only a very few boys did not adopt their father's job. For girls, there were virtually no choices. They married, as directed and provided children to continue the family traditions. Entering a religious order was virtually the only other alternative.

But in America, it was different. In America, there were choices. Admittedly options were more restricted. In America, there were choices. Admittedly, options were more restricted in the cities of the Colonies, but the free-spirited could flee convention and set out for the frontier. With the passing of time, more choices opened in Europe, but America still is, as it has always been, the world's land of choice.

An extensive publicly supported education system is free for taking in America. Students who choose to do so can learn almost anything they wish, and the Scottish Rite is rightfully proud of its part in providing scholarship support to worthy students. Any capable student can be educated for virtually any profession. It is a matter of motivation and personal choice.

In America, you choose your life's work, your place of residence, your friends and associates, and the partner with whom to share your life. In contrast, the lives of countless men and women around the world still depend more upon chance than choice. There is a price, a high price, to be paid for choice. That price is responsibility. The very fact that we can choose means we are responsible for the consequences of our choices. It is always easier to have someone choose for you. Making choices means confronting uncertainty and risking the possibility of failure. If your life is ruled by chance, you can always shift the blame to others. Giving up free will is always tempting. Around the globe, dictators, accepted by their people, still rule.

Albert Pike understood this when he wrote, "It is only by unwearying patience and unremitting exertion that even the most intelligent people can be prevented from throwing away its heritage of freedom. ... The eras of true freedom, brief and transitory, have been only the dreams of the world." But if freedom is a dream, that dream is American. We have chosen the harder path, and that choice has made us the great nation we are.

America chooses to be great.

C. Fred Kleinknecht

Made in the USA
Middletown, DE
05 October 2022